JAPANESE

Verbs

& Essentials
of Grammar

Titles available in this series:

JAPANESE

Verbs

& Essentials of Grammar

Third Edition

Rita L. Lampkin

New York Chicago San Francisco Lisbon London Madrid Mexico City
Milan New Delhi San Juan Seoul Singapore Sydney Toronto

Library of Congress Cataloging-in-Publication Data

Lampkin, R. (Rita)
    Japanese verbs & essentials of grammar / Rita L. Lampkin. — 3rd ed.
       p.   cm.
    Includes index.
    ISBN 0-07-171363-8
    1. Japanese language—Verb.   2. Japanese language—Grammar.   3. Japanese
language—Textbooks for foreign speakers—English.   I. Title.   II. Japanese verbs
and essentials of grammar.

    PL585.L26   2010
    496'.56—dc22   2009051797

1 2 3 4 5 6 7 8 9 10 11 12 13 14 15   WFR/WFR   1 9 8 7 6 5 4 3 2 1 0

ISBN 978-0-07-171363-4
MHID   0-07-171363-8

McGraw-Hill books are available at special quantity discounts to use as premiums and
sales promotions or for use in corporate training programs. To contact a representative,
please e-mail us at bulksales@mcgraw-hill.com.

Bonus Audio Download

A bonus audio recording for this book can be obtained from mhprofessional.com. Simply
follow these easy steps:

1. Go to mhprofessional.com.
2. Search for *Japanese Verbs & Essentials of Grammar*.
3. Locate "Downloads" underneath the book's cover image.
4. Select story link to listen and/or download.

Preface

Japanese Verbs and Essentials of Grammar is a practical handbook and guide to the principal grammatical concepts of the Japanese language for learners at any level of proficiency. Concepts are presented in a logical order and concise manner so that even beginning students can follow the explanations. More advanced students will also find this an excellent quick reference and review guide.

All grammatical explanations are given in layman's language, so as to be understandable to students of any age, from junior high upwards. This book can be used as a basis for group work, individual study, or simply as a classroom or personal reference.

Part One focuses on Japanese verbs. The chapter on pronunciation at the beginning of the section gives a good introduction for beginners to the sounds of the language. In subsequent chapters the differences between Western and Japanese verb concepts is expounded clearly and simply, with example sentences in contemporary, usable Japanese given for each verb ending presented.

Part Two offers concise explanations of other essential points of grammar, including particles, "Ko-so-a-do" words, adjective conjugations, counters, and other principles peculiar to Japanese. In all cases particular attention is paid to the English-speaking learner's point of view, answering the questions that invariably come up as a result of the differences between the two languages. Part Two also includes a helpful reference section that lists common idiomatic phrases, place names, and vocabulary items of interest to both the beginning learner and the more advanced student. Japanese written characters, punctuation basics, information on holidays, and some pertinent historical data are presented in two appendices, along with a selection of interesting Japanese literary proverbs.

For classwork or for personal reference, *Japanese Verbs and Essentials of Grammar* is a versatile and easy-to-use guide. It is a helpful tool for learners seeking not only to understand verb usage and grammar points but also to gain a practical working knowledge of Japanese.

Acknowledgment

It would be nice to be able to say, "I wrote this book all by myself," but that would be deceptive. Although the words are mine, and I certainly spent a lot of hours in research and a lot of thought, effort, and perspiration bringing the book to fruition, I have to acknowledge the invaluable assistance of Mr. Osamu Hoshino of Salt Lake City, Utah, who also spent countless hours going over my work to make sure that it conforms with the realities of current Japanese.

A native of Japan, Mr. Hoshino has over two decades of experience teaching Japanese in the U.S. and English in Japan, as well as developing course materials for both languages. He holds an MPA degree from Brigham Young University and serves the State of Utah in the area of economic development, which requires him to be in close contact with Japan, its people, language, and culture. He also has great support from his wife Fumiko and three growing children.

It is to him and his family that I extend my personal gratitude and dedicate this work.

–Rita L. Lampkin

Contents

Part One:
Japanese Verbs

1. Romanization & Pronunciation

The Roman alphabet (called **rōmaji** in Japanese) is used to represent the Japanese language for English-speaking students who are not yet familiar with the Japanese writing system.

There are several forms of **rōmaji** or "romanization" in use; the system used in this book follows that found in most of the romanized Japanese-English dictionaries currently published in Japan.

For the benefit of those who may be more familiar with other forms of **rōmaji**, following is a list of the major differences between the system used in *Japanese Verbs and Essentials of Grammar* and other common systems.

JVEG	OTHERS	JVEG	OTHERS
sha	sya	zu	du / dzu
shi	si	fu	hu
shu	syu	o / (w)o	wo
sho	syo	nm	mm
ja	jya / zya / dya	nb	mb
ji	di / zi	np	mp
ju	jyu / zyu / dyu	ā	aa
jo	jyo / zyo / dyo	ū	uu
chi	ti	ē	ee
tsu	tu	ō	oo
tch	cch		

Also, an apostrophe (') is placed after the single-syllable consonant **n** when it comes before a vowel or **ya, yu,** or **yo,** in order to distinguish it from the syllables **na, ni, nu, ne, no** and **nya, nyu, nyo.** For example, the word **hon'ya** has three syllables: **ho - n - ya.**

Vowels

There are only five vowel sounds in Japanese:

/a/	as in f<u>a</u>ther
/i/	as in mach<u>i</u>ne
/u/	as in rec<u>u</u>perate
/e/	as in s<u>e</u>t
/o/	as in c<u>o</u>operate

These vowel sounds are always short in duration (unless specifically elongated, as described below), and they are never diphthongized in standard Japanese.

A "long vowel" is simply a repetition of the same vowel sound, as in the words **okāsan** (o-ka-a-sa-n), **jū** (ju-u), **onēsan** (o-ne-e-sa-n), **Ōsaka** (o-o-sa-ka). In this book these are indicated by a macron over the elongated vowel, except in the case of the long **i**, which is doubled (**oniisan, ureshii**) for typographical clarity and convenience.

The vowels **a, e,** and **o** are always pronounced distinctly in Japanese. The vowels **i** and **u**, however, are sometimes not vocalized, particularly when they occur between two unvoiced consonants (**k, s, sh, t, ch, h, f, p**) or at the end of a word. A word like **hito**, for example, will be pronounced as if there is no **i** (**h'to**), **watakushi** is pronounced **watak'shi**, and verbs that end in -**masu** are often pronounced without the final **u**. This is especially true in male speech, as well as in casual speech for both male and female speakers.

Consonants

The Japanese language has almost no consonant clusters, but consists primarily of syllables made up of either a vowel alone, a consonant-and-vowel combination, or a single consonant. Because of this characteristic, the phonetic writing systems of Japanese are arranged not in an alphabet, but in a "syllabary," each character representing one syllable. Following is the romanized version of the Japanese syllabary. *(See Appendix A for the Japanese characters.)*

The Japanese Syllabary

A	I	U	E	O	
KA	KI	KU	KE	KO	
GA	GI	GU	GE	GO	
SA	SHI	SU	SE	SO	
ZA	JI	ZU	ZE	ZO	
TA	CHI	TSU	TE	TO	
DA	JI	ZU	DE	DO	
NA	NI	NU	NE	NO	
HA	HI	FU	HE	HO	
BA	BI	BU	BE	BO	
PA	PI	PU	PE	PO	
MA	MI	MU	ME	MO	
YA	–	YU	–	YO	
RA	RI	RU	RE	RO	
WA	–	–	–	(w)O	N / N'

Also possible are certain "combination syllables," as follows:

KYA	KYU	KYO		HYA	HYU	HYO
GYA	GYU	GYO		BYA	BYU	BYO
SHA	SHU	SHO		PYA	PYU	PYO
CHA	CHU	CHO		MYA	MYU	MYO
JA	JU	JO		RYA	RYU	RYO
NYA	NYU	NYO				

Single-Consonant Syllables

The single-consonant syllable **n (n')** is represented by its own character as part of the basic syllabary. As shown in the following examples, it occurs in the middle and at the end of words, but never at the beginning of a word.

kin *(gold)*   **Kin'yōbi** *(Friday)*
san *(three)*   **sanmyaku** *(mountain range)*

It is possible, as well, to create a single-consonant syllable by doubling certain consonant sounds, specifically **k**, **s/sh**, **t/ch**, and **p**, as in the following:

hakkiri *(clear)*   **massugu** *(straight)*   **nesshin** *(eager)*
mottomo *(most)*   **itchi** *(agreement)*   **suppai** *(sour)*

Note that only the consonants mentioned above are doubled, and that they are all unvoiced consonants. Voiced consonants (**g**, **z**, **d**, **j**, and **b**) are not doubled except in words of foreign origin; eg, **hotto doggu** *(hot dog)*, **beddo** *(bed)*. Voiced consonants in Japanese words are never doubled.

Japanese vs. English Consonants

Most Japanese consonants are pronounced essentially the same as in English, with the following exceptions:

TS   Although this sound occurs in English, it never comes at the beginning of a word, as it frequently does in Japanese, except in a borrowed word, such as **tsunami** *(tidal wave)*. In Japanese this sound is always followed by the vowel **u**.

F   This sound is more open than the English **f**. It is made with the lower lip not quite touching the upper teeth and has been described as being "halfway between an **f** and an **h**." In Japanese words it is always followed by the vowel **u**.

R Although romanized with an **r**, this sound is closer to an **l**, but only the tip of the tongue (not the flattened end as when making an **l**) is tapped against the ridge behind the upper teeth, farther back than when making a **t** or a **d**. Also, it is never rolled or trilled as in Spanish, but is always a single tap.

W There are two occasions when this sound occurs in Japanese: in the syllable **wa** and in the syllable **(w)o**. In **wa** the **w** is about the same as in English; however, in the syllable **(w)o**, it is much softer and frequently is eliminated altogether. For the beginning student, it is acceptable to omit the **w** in front of **o**, pronouncing this syllable exactly like the **o** of **a-i-u-e-o**.

N This sound is softer and more nasalized than the **n** of **na-ni-nu-ne-no**. Before **b, p**, or **m** it is pronounced more or less like an **m**; before **na, ni, nu, ne**, or **no** it is hardened to match the initial **n** of those syllables.

Intonation

Japanese is called a "monotonic" language, which means that it does not have the up-and-down tones that are characteristic of Chinese, Vietnamese, and some other Asian languages. It also does not require accent or emphasis on a particular syllable of a word, as in English and other Western languages.

This monotonic quality, however, does not mean that Japanese is spoken in a flat monotone, with no intonation whatever; on the contrary, intonation and emphasis are common in Japanese speech, varying, of course, from speaker to speaker according to the particular conversational situation and context. There are also regional dialects with varying pronunciation, intonation, and vocabulary/grammar habits, just as there are elsewhere.

2. The Japanese Writing System

There are three kinds of Japanese written characters: **kanji, katakana,** and **hiragana**.

Kanji characters are ideographs and pictographs borrowed from the Chinese. Each character has a certain general meaning, but it may be pronounced several different ways, depending on the specific intended meaning and how the word is used in the sentence. There are over 1900 **kanji** in common use. Many of the Chinese characters have been modified over the years by the Japanese, either to accommodate the differences in the two languages or just to simplify the writing.

Katakana and **hiragana** characters are strictly phonetic; that is, each character represents a certain syllable of sound without respect to meaning. Collectively, these characters are called **kana**.

Each of the two phonetic systems represents the same set of syllables. **Hiragana** has a more flowing, cursive look than **katakana**, but the real difference between the two systems is in usage.

Words of non-Japanese origin (except Chinese words that have become accepted as Japanese) are written in **katakana. Katakana** is also frequently used to add emphasis or call attention to a word, so it is widely used in advertising and other special applications.

Hiragana is used to write verb endings, particles and other grammatical tools, and any word for which there is no **kanji** or the writer does not know the **kanji**.

There is no such thing as capitalization of Japanese characters, and the use of punctuation is limited. *(See Appendix A.)*

Traditionally, Japanese was written vertically, beginning in the upper right. Modern Japanese may be written either horizontally (usually left to right) or vertically. Books that deal with math, science, music, foreign languages, and the like, are written horizontally to accommodate Western writing conventions, such as Arabic numerals and scientific symbols; novels and other books are usually written vertically. Names, information or advertisements written on the sides of vehicles are normally written horizontally from the front of the vehicle toward the rear; therefore, the information will be left-to-right on one side of the car and right-to-left on the other. Also, Chinese apothecaries or restaurants may have signs written from right to left, Chinese style.

A common question among beginning Japanese learners is why phonetic characters are not used exclusively, eliminating the more difficult **kanji** system.

Aside from the obvious logistical problems involved in changing the writing system of millions of people, the main obstacle to this has to do with the limited number of sounds and sound combinations in Japanese, which has resulted in the creation—with the normal changes in the language over the centuries, plus extensive borrowing from the Chinese—of many words that sound alike but have different meanings.

It is the **kanji** for each word that distinguishes it from others that sound like it. For this reason, even in oral conversation, the Japanese will often refer to the appropriate **kanji** or "write" the **kanji** with the finger of one hand on the palm of the other to clarify meaning for the listener.

(See Appendix A for examples of all three Japanese writing systems.)

3. General Information on Verbs

The difficulty that many Western students face in learning Japanese lies primarily in the fact that it is very *different* from languages that are more familiar to them; however, there are certain characteristics about Japanese verbs that make them actually *simpler* to use and manipulate than Western languages. More detailed information is given later in this book, but below are some basic principles that should be given special consideration.

- The Japanese verb *always* comes at the end of the sentence.
- The verb *does not change* for person, number or gender.
- There are only two irregular verbs and few irregularities in other verbs.
- There are only two basic tenses: past and present. Future intention is indicated by the present tense, which is sometimes called the "non-past."

Dictionary Form

The Dictionary Form is the verb as it is found in a dictionary. It corresponds in some ways with the English "infinitive," but in other ways is quite different. The Dictionary Form always ends in the vowel **u**.

Levels of Speech

In most languages there is a marked difference between the way a person will speak in casual situations and under more formal conditions. In Japanese these differences are formalized into several fairly distinct styles of speech. Generally, they can be classified into four levels:

- **Abrupt**—used when speaking "down" to children, animals, or other social inferiors;
- **Informal**—used when speaking with close friends, family members, or peers in a casual situation;
- **Normal-polite**—(also called the **Desu-masu** Form) used when speaking with strangers, business associates, and others when courtesy is called for;
- **Honorific**—used in very formal situations or when speaking to superiors, clients, etc.

The differences between the levels show up in choice of vocabulary, verb endings and other grammatical constructions. There is a degree of acceptable overlap between the levels of speech, as well as certain traditional Honorific expressions that may be used at any level (greetings, apologies, etc.). Informal verb endings are also freely used in "Impersonal" speech, such as broadcast news, formal announcements, etc.

Examples used in this book are primarily in the Normal-polite range, except where other levels are explained or otherwise called for. The Informal level is treated in Chapter 18, *The Informal Form*, and Honorific speech is introduced in Chapter 37, *Honorifics*. Occasional references are made to certain common Abrupt forms; otherwise, that level is not treated in this book.

4. Kinds of Verbs

Irregular

There are only two irregular verbs in Japanese: **kuru** *(come)* and **suru** *(do)*. **Suru** often occurs in two-word verbs such as **benkyō suru** *(study)* and **unten suru** *(drive)*. Also, frequently a phrase that includes a direct object will be treated as a two-word verb, with the object particle **o** omitted; eg, **denwa [o] suru** *(to telephone)* and **kaimono [o] suru** *(shop, do the shopping)*.

Ichidan
("Vowel-stem")

In the Dictionary Form Ichidan verbs all end in either **-iru** or **-eru**. Following is a list of some common Ichidan verbs and their meanings.

ageru *(raise, lift up; give)*   **kiru** *(put on [clothes], wear)*
deru *(leave, exit, go out)*   **miru** *(see, watch, look)*
hareru *(clear up)*   **ochiru** *(fall, come/go down)*
iru *(be located)*   **taberu** *(eat)*

Yodan
("Consonant-stem")

All verbs that are not Irregular or Ichidan are in this category. In the Dictionary Form Yodan verbs may end in one of nine syllables: **-u, -tsu, -ru, -ku, -gu, -su, -nu, -mu,** or **-bu**. For our purposes Yodan verbs that end in the syllable **u** in the Dictionary Form (eg. **kau**) will be called **U-verbs**, verbs that end in **ku** (eg. **aruku**) will be **KU-verbs**, etc.

Following are some common Yodan verbs and their meanings.

U-verbs: au *(meet)*, **iu** *(say, tell)*, **kau** *(buy)*, **omou** *(think/opine)*, **utau** *(sing)*

TSU-verbs: katsu *(win)*, **matsu** *(wait)*, **motsu** *(own; hold)*, **tatsu** *(stand up)*

RU-verbs: hairu* *(enter)*, **owaru** *(end)*, **suwaru** *(sit down)*, **wakaru** *(understand)*

KU-verbs: aru<u>ku</u> *(walk)*, ha<u>ku</u> *(put on [footwear])*, ka<u>ku</u> *(write)*, ugo<u>ku</u> *(move)*

GU-verbs: ao<u>gu</u> *(gaze, stare)*, iso<u>gu</u> *(hurry)*, nu<u>gu</u> *(remove)*, oyo<u>gu</u> *(swim)*

SU-verbs: da<u>su</u> *(send)*, hana<u>su</u> *(speak)*, ke<u>su</u> *(erase)*, o<u>su</u> *(push)*, ta<u>su</u> *(add)*

NU-verbs: shi<u>nu</u> *(die)* [There are no other NU-verbs.]

MU-verbs: no<u>mu</u> *(drink)*, su<u>mu</u> *(reside)*, tano<u>mu</u> *(request)*, yasu<u>mu</u> *(rest)*

BU-verbs: aso<u>bu</u> *(play)*, era<u>bu</u> *(choose)*, hako<u>bu</u> *(carry)*, to<u>bu</u> *(fly)*, yo<u>bu</u> *(call)*

*NOTE that there are a few Yodan verbs that look like Ichidan verbs in the Dictionary Form. These exceptional Yodan verbs include the following:

chiru *(fall, scatter)*	**keru** *(kick)*
hairu *(enter)*	**kiru** *(cut)*
hashiru *(run)*	**mairu** *(come/go [humble])*
iru *(need)*	**nigiru** *(grasp)*
kaeru *(return)*	**shiru** *(know)*
kagiru *(limit)*	**shaberu** *(talk, chat)*

5. <u>Desu</u>

Although **desu**, meaning "to be" or "to equal," is probably the most common Japanese verb, it is so different from other verbs that it is most often treated as a separate entity.

The usual sentence pattern for this verb is **[A] wa [B] desu**, where **[A]** is the topic or thing under discussion and **[B]** is one of the following:

1. a **definition**—a noun or noun phrase telling what the topic *is*

    Ex.: <u>Kore</u> wa <u>pen</u> desu. *This is a pen.*
         [A]   [B]

         <u>Kanojo</u> wa <u>kinō kita hito</u> desu. *She is the person who*
         [A]   [B]   *came yesterday.*

2. a **description** —an adjective or adjective phrase telling what something *is like*

    Ex.: <u>Ano hon</u> wa <u>yomiyasui</u> desu. *That book is easy to read.*
         [A]   [B]

         <u>Apāto</u> wa <u>eki ni benri</u> desu. *The apartment is convenient*
         [A]   [B]   *to the train station.*

3. a **relative location word** such as **koko, soko, asoko, mukō** or **doko**—telling where something *is located*

    Ex.: <u>Rajio</u> wa <u>koko</u> desu. *The radio is [over] here.*
         [A]   [B]

         <u>Toshokan</u> wa <u>doko</u> desu ka? *Where is the library?*
         [A]   [B]

Basic conjugations of **desu** are as follows:

desu	present positive *(am, are, is)*
dewa arimasen	present negative *(am not, are not, is not)*
deshita	past positive *(was, were)*
dewa arimasen deshita	past negative *(was not, were not)*

In casual speech **dewa** is often contracted to **ja (ja arimasen, ja arimasen deshita)**; however, in this book the standard form **dewa** is used.

6. Verbs in a Sentence

As it is used in a sentence, a verb can be broken down into three parts: the **stem**, the **base**, and the **ending**.

Stem

The **stem** of a verb is the part that gives the *general action* or meaning; that is, "walk," "do," "sing," "hear," "be," etc.

The stem of Yodan and Ichidan verbs is what is left after removing the last syllable of the Dictionary Form. For example, the stem of **hataraku** *(work)* is **hatara-**, the stem of **taberu** *(eat)* is **tabe-**, the stem of **iru** *(be located)* is **i-**, etc.

Except for irregular verbs **kuru** *(come)* and **suru** *(do)*, the stem of a verb never changes. The stems of **kuru** and **suru** change with each base, and it is this that gives them their irregular quality.

Base

The **base** *links* the stem of the verb with the ending. All possible bases are given in the verb chart in Chapter 7. Bases have no intrinsic meaning, but simply link the stem of the verb to the verb ending. However, use of the wrong base for a particular verb or verb ending can result in miscommunication or cause confusion for the listener.

The choice of which base to use in a given verb situation is made according to two criteria:

1. The *row* choice (from the verb chart) is dictated by the Dictionary Form of the verb. For example, if the verb ends in **ku** in the Dictionary Form (eg, **kaku, kiku, aruku**), the base must be chosen from the **ka-ki-ku-ke-kō-ite-ita** row.

2. The base category (Base 1, 2, 3, etc.—*columns* in the verb chart) is dictated by the verb ending. For example, the ending **-mashita** (past tense) requires Base 2. Since all **KU**-verbs change to **ki** in Base 2, **kaku** *(to write)* would become **kakimashita** *([I] wrote)*, **aruku** *(to walk)* would be **arukimashita** *([I] walked)*, **iku** *(to go)* would be **ikimashita** *([I] went)*, etc.

For further examples of the choice and use of bases, see Chapters 9-18.

Ending

The **verb ending** gives the *specific function* of the verb; ie, past or present tense, negative or positive, plus many other functions. For example, for the verb **kaku** *(to write),* the ending **-masu** indicates *[I] write* or *[I] will write;* **-tai desu** tells *[I] want to write;* **-hazu desu** indicates *[I] am supposed to write;* **-nai to omoimasu** means *[I] think [I] won't write;* etc.

A number of the more common verb endings are presented later in this book. *Each ending may be attached to the stem of any verb by means of a particular base.* A verb ending should be memorized with its proper base.

7. Verb Base Chart

The chart below presents all possible verb bases, using 13 example verbs. *All* Japanese verbs (except **desu**) are represented by these examples. That is, all U-verbs will use the same bases as **kau**, all KU-verbs use the same bases as **kaku**, all Ichidan verbs use the same bases as **taberu** and **miru**, etc.

	Example verbs	Stem	Bases: 1	2	3	4	5	(6) TE-Form	(7) TA-Form
Yodan Verbs	kau *(buy)*	ka-	wa	i	u	e	ō	tte	tta
	matsu *(wait)*	ma-	ta	chi	tsu	te	tō	tte	tta
	shiru *(know)*	shi-	ra	ri	ru	re	rō	tte	tta
	kaku *(write)*	ka-	ka	ki	ku	ke	kō	ite	ita
	oyogu *(swim)*	oyo-	ga	gi	gu	ge	gō	ide	ida
	hanasu *(speak)*	hana-	sa	shi	su	se	sō	shite	shita
	shinu *(die)*	shi-	na	ni	nu	ne	nō	nde	nda
	yomu *(read)*	yo-	ma	mi	mu	me	mō	nde	nda
	asobu *(play)*	aso-	ba	bi	bu	be	bō	nde	nda
Ichidan	taberu *(eat)*	tabe-	—	—	ru	re	yō	te	ta
	miru *(see)*	mi-	—	—	ru	re	yō	te	ta
Irregular	kuru *(come)*	—	ko	ki	kuru	kure / kore	koyō	kite	kita
	suru *(do)*	—	shi	shi	suru	sure	shiyō	shite	shita

For Ichidan verbs, since there is no Base 1 or 2, any ending that calls for those bases must be attached directly to the stem.

Note that there are two forms of Base 4 for **kuru**. The verb ending dictates which of the two should be used.

8. The <u>Masu</u> Form

A major staple of the Normal-polite level of speech is a set of verb endings collectively called the **Masu Form**. **Masu Form** endings and their functions are:

-masu	present or future tense ("non-past")
-mashita	past tense
-masen	negative present or future
-masen deshita	negative past
-mashō	inclusive command: *Let's* . . .

Use of the **Masu Form** creates a simple indicative statement, with the exception of the inclusive command ending **-mashō**. Adding **ka** after any ending makes the statement into a question. The ending **-mashō ka** (inclusive query) is translated *Shall we . . . ?*

The **Masu Form** is always attached to a verb with Base 2 *(see Verb Base Chart on previous page)*. Following are examples of Yodan and Ichidan verbs, plus Irregular verbs **kuru** and **suru**, as they occur in the **Masu Form**. (Remember that verbs do not change for person, number or gender of the subject.)

Yodan: **kaku** *(to write)*

kakimasu *(write/writes/will write)*
kakimashita *(wrote)*
kakimasen *(don't write/won't write)*
kakimasen deshita *(didn't write)*
kakimashō *(Let's write.)*

Ichidan: **taberu** *(to eat)*

tabemasu *(eat/eats/will eat)*
tabemashita *(ate)*
tabemasen *(don't eat/won't eat)*
tabemasen deshita *(didn't eat)*
tabemashō *(Let's eat.)*

Irregular:
kuru *(to come)*

kimasu *(come/comes/will come)*
kimashita *(came)*
kimasen *(don't come/won't come)*
kimasen deshita *(didn't come)*
kimashō *(Let's come.)*

suru *(to do)*

shimasu *(do/does/will do)*
shimashita *(did)*
shimasen *(don't do/won't do)*
shimasen deshita *(didn't do)*
shimashō *(Let's do.)*

9. Verb Endings

General Information

Beginning in Chapter 10 is a listing of verb endings in common daily use, grouped according to which base each ending requires. Verb endings not included here are either less commonly used in current Japanese or are considered beyond the scope of this book.

Each ending is listed with its grammatical function/approximate English counterpart, example sentences, exceptional or idiomatic situations, and other information as appropriate.

At the beginning of each section of this list is a portion of the Verb Base Chart that includes all the example verbs from the full chart *(page 14)*, along with their **Stem + Base** forms. There is also a brief explanation of each base, notes on exceptional functions, and other pertinent information.

Terminology

Hereafter, a verb in a particular base will be referred to as follows:

Stem + Base 1 = **V1**   *Stem + Base 5* = **V5**
Stem + Base 2 = **V2**   *Stem + Base 6* = **V6 or TE-form**
Stem + Base 3 = **V3**   *Stem + Base 7* = **V7 or TA-form**
Stem + Base 4 = **V4**

Characteristics

Auxiliary/New Verbs: Many verb endings employ auxiliary verbs, such as **iru, aru**, and **dekiru**, or create entirely new verbs, such as **yomeru, mōshikomu, kaeritagaru**, all of which follow the same conjugational patterns as simple verb forms.

For example, **mōshikomu** in the **Masu Form** follows the pattern of any **MU-verb: mōshikomimasu, mōshikomimashita, mōshikomimasen**, etc. **Yomeru** follows the pattern of all Ichidan verbs: **yomemasu, yomemashita**, and so on. The verb phrase **kaku koto ga aru** follows the conjugational pattern of **arimasu: arimashita, arimasen**, etc.

Combining Endings: In many cases it is possible to combine verb endings; for example, **mi ni iku** *(go to see)* plus **ikitai desu** *(want to go)* becomes **mi ni ikitai desu** *(want to go to see)*.

Adjective Endings: Some verb endings make the verb into an adjective phrase, which will follow the conjugational patterns of adjectives. *(See Chapter 25, Adjectives.)* For example, **V2 + tai** is a True Adjective form and is so conjugated: **-takatta** (past), **-takunai** (negative), **-takunakatta** (negative past). **V2 + sō**, however, creates a Quasi Adjective: **taoresō na hito** *(the person who looks like he's going to collapse),* **ame ga furisō na sora** *(a sky that looks like it's going to rain).*

Endings for <u>DESU</u>

   Many of the verb endings listed in this section are also used after some form of the verb **desu**; in such cases, appropriate examples are given. Other endings are rarely or never used after **desu** in current Japanese.

   It should be noted that in many cases **naru** *(become)* is more appropriate than **desu**. For example, in Japanese a person would not say, "I want to be a teacher" (using **desu**), but instead would say, "I want to *become* a teacher" **(Sensei ni naritai desu)**, using the verb **naru**.

10. Base 1 Endings

Ex. Verbs	V1
Yodan	
kau	kawa-
matsu	mata-
shiru	shira-
kaku	kaka-
oyogu	oyoga-
hanasu	hanasa-
shinu	shina-
yomu	yoma-
asobu	asoba-
Ichidan	
taberu	tabe-
miru	mi-
Irregular	
kuru	ko-
suru	shi-

Base 1 is sometimes called the "Negative Base," because most of the endings that require Base 1 have some negative aspect.

Note that all Yodan verbs have a Base 1 form with the vowel **a**. Ichidan verbs have no Base 1; therefore, any V1 ending is attached directly to the stem of an Ichidan verb.

Following is a selection of common V1 endings.

-nai [desu]   Informal negative: *do not, will not. (Cf. V2 + masen.)*
Following **-nai** with **desu** raises the level of the sentence from Casual to the Normal-polite range without altering meaning.

Ex.: **Eigo ga wakaranai.** *(Casual)*
[I] don't understand English.
Nihonshoku wa tabenai desu.
[He] doesn't eat Japanese food.

Exception: **aru (arimasu)** becomes **-nai.**

Ex.: **Okane ga nai desu.** *[I] don't have any money.*

Desu with this ending becomes **dewanai** or **janai. Dewanai** is not usually followed by **desu**, although the more colloquial **janai** often is.

Ex.: **Watashi no dewanai.** or **Watashi no janai desu.**
It is not mine.

-naide   *without doing, without having done*

Shukudai o shinaide, gakkō ni dekakete shimaimashita.
He went off to school without doing his homework.

-naide kudasai   Negative request: *Please don't.*

Ex.: **Koko de tabako o nomanaide kudasai.**
Please don't smoke here.

-nakatta [desu]   Informal negative past: *did not. (Cf. V2 + masen deshita.)*
Following **-nakatta** with **desu** raises the level of the sentence from Casual
to the Normal-polite range without altering meaning.

Ex.: **Eigo ga wakaranakatta.** *(Casual)*
[I] didn't understand English.
O-tomodachi wa kinō konakatta desu.
Your friend did not come yesterday.

Exception: **aru (arimashita)** becomes **nakatta [desu]**.

Ex.: **Okane ga nakatta desu.** *[I] didn't have any money.*

Desu becomes **dewanakatta** or **janakatta**. **Dewanakatta** is not usually
followed by **desu**, although the more colloquial **janakatta** often is.

Ex.: **Watakushi no dewanakatta.** or **Watashi no janakatta desu.**
It was not mine.

-nakattara   Conditional negative: *If/when [I] don't/didn't*

Ex.: **Ikanakattara, okāsan wa okoru deshō.**
If I didn't go, Mother would probably get angry.

Exceptional: **aru** becomes **nakattara**.

Ex.: **Okane ga nakattara, komaru to omoimasu.**
I think I'd be in trouble if I didn't have any money.

Desu: **dewanakattara** or **janakattara**

Watakushi no dewanakattara, tsukaimasen.
I wouldn't use it if it weren't mine.

-nakereba   Conditional negative: *If [I] don't*

Ex.: **Kikanakereba wakarimasen.**
You won't know if you don't ask.
O-tomodachi ga konakereba, denwa o shite kudasai.
If your friend doesn't come, phone me.

Exceptional: **aru** becomes **nakereba**.

Ex. **Okane ga nakereba komarimasu.**
If you don't have any money, it'll be a problem.

Desu: **denakereba**

Ex.: **Kaiin denakereba, haitte wa ikemasen.**
If you are not a member, you can't go in.

-nakereba narimasen   Obligational: *must, have to*

Ex.: **Kaeranakereba narimasen.**   *I have to go back.*

Exceptional: **aru** becomes **nakereba narimasen.**

Ex.: **Okane ga nakereba narimasen.**   *You have to have money.*

Desu: **denakereba narimasen**

Ex.: **Juppun ijō denakereba narimasen.**
    It has to be more than ten minutes.

-nakute   TE-form of Informal negative **-nai:** *without doing, not doing; does not do and . . .*

Ex.: **O-kyakusan ga konakute, dō shimasu ka?**
    What will you do if your guest does not come? (Lit. Your guest does not come, and what do you do?)

Often used to negate one idea and affirm another *(not this, but that).*

Ex.: **Tegami o kakanakute, denwa o shimashita.**
    I didn't write a letter; I telephoned.

Exceptional: **aru** becomes **nakute.**

Ex.: **Okane ga nakute, kaimasen deshita.**
    I didn't have any money, [so] I didn't buy it.

Desu: **dewanakute** or **janakute.**

Ex.: **Nihonjin dewanakute, Chūgokujin desu.**
    He is not Japanese; he is Chinese.

-nakute mo   *Even if [I] don't*

Ex.: **Kaisha ni ikanakute mo, shigoto ga arimasu.**
    Even if I don't go to the company, I [still] have to work.

Exceptional: **aru** becomes **nakute mo.**

Ex.: **Kuruma ga nakute mo, ikanakereba narimasen.**
    Even if you don't have a car, you have to go.

Desu: **de[wa]nakute mo** or **janakute mo**

Ex.: **Sensei dewanakute mo, shitte imasu.**
    He knows, even though he is not a teacher.

-nakute mo ii [desu]   *It's okay not to*

Ex.: **Wasabi o tabenakute mo ii desu.**
    It's okay not to eat the horseradish sauce.

Exceptional: **aru** becomes **nakute mo ii [desu].**

Ex.: **Kuruma ga nakute mo ii desu.**   *It's okay not to have a car.*

Desu: de[wa]nakute mo ii or janakute mo ii [desu]

Ex.: **Yuri denakute mo ii desu.**
It's okay if it is not a lily. (Another flower will do.)

-nakute [wa] ikemasen/dame desu   Obligational: *must, have to*

Ex.: **Sanji ni kusuri o nomanakute wa ikemasen.**
I have to take medicine at 3:00.
Otōsan mo konakute wa dame desu.
Your father has to come, too.

Exceptional: **aru** becomes **nakute** . . .

Ex.: **Denwa ga nakute wa ikemasen.** *You have to have a phone.*

Desu: de[wa]nakute . . .   janakute . . .

Ex.: **Akai bara denakute wa dame desu.** *They have to be red roses.*

-reru/rareru   Passive: *be done.* **-reru** is used with Yodan verbs, **-rareru** with Ichidan verbs. Irregular verbs become **korareru** and **sareru.** The agent of the action is followed by **ni.**

Ex.: **Saifu wa dorobō ni nusumaremashita.**
The wallet was stolen by a thief.
Kare wa minna ni shirarete imasu.
He is known by everyone.
Sensei ni shitsumon saremashita.
I was asked a question by the teacher.

Potential/Passive (Ichidan verbs): *can do, can be done*

Ex.: **Otōsan wa sashimi ga taberaremasen.**
My father cannot eat raw fish. (Lit. As for my father, raw fish cannot be eaten.)
Itsudemo tabako o yamerareru to omoimasu.
I think I can quit [smoking] cigarettes any time.

Exceptional: **miru** *(see)* in the Potential/Passive Form becomes **mieru** *(be visible). (See V4 + ru.)*

Honorific *(See Chapter 36, Honorifics.)*

-seru/saseru   Causative: *make [someone] do, let [someone] do.* **-seru** is used with Yodan verbs, **-saseru** with Ichidan. Irregular verbs become **kosaseru** and **saseru.**

Ex.: **Okāsan wa kodomo ni kusuri o nomasemashita.**
The mother made the child take the medicine.
Kachō ga watakushi ni hanashi o sasete kuremashita.
The section chief [kindly] allowed me to speak.

-zu ni   *without doing.* Irregular verbs become **kozu** and **sezu**.

> Ex.: **Nanimo iwazu ni nakidashimashita.**
> *Without saying a word, he started crying.*
> **Benkyō sezu ni gakkō ni dekakemashita.**
> *He went off to school without studying.*

11. Base 2 Endings

Ex. Verbs	V2
Yodan	
kau	kai-
matsu	machi-
shiru	shiri-
kaku	kaki-
oyogu	oyogi-
hanasu	hanashi-
shinu	shini-
yomu	yomi-
asobu	asobi-
Ichidan	
taberu	tabe-
miru	mi-
Irregular	
kuru	ki-
suru	shi-

Base 2 is sometimes called the "Noun-forming Base," since V2 with no ending can act as a noun, or the "Continuative Base," since it can also indicate that another verb will follow in the sentence.

Also, V2 followed by **mono** *(thing)* makes a new noun that relates to the action of the verb; for example, the Base 2 form of **taberu** *(eat)* + **mono** becomes **tabemono** *(food/things to eat).*

Note that all Yodan verbs have a Base 2 form with the vowel **i**. Ichidan verbs have no Base 2; therefore, a V2 ending is attached directly to the stem of the verb.

Following is a selection of common V2 endings.

[No ending]   Makes a verb into a noun.

    Ex.: **Kare no <u>hanashi</u> wa chotto shinjiraremasen.**
        I find it hard to believe his story (what he says).
    Shōsetsu no <u>hajime</u> wa ichiban taisetsu desu.
        The beginning of the novel is the most important.

[No ending]   Continuation Form. Indicates that at least one other verb follows. "And" can be included in translation. This usage gives a more formal or literary flavor to the sentence than the TE-form as Continuation. *(See Chapter 15.)*

    Ex.: **O-tegami o <u>yomi</u>, sugu ni henji o kakimashita.**
        I read your letter and immediately wrote a reply.
    Yūshoku o <u>tabe</u>, ato wa oboete imasen.
        I ate dinner, and [what happened] afterwards I don't remember.

Desu: deari

    Kyōto wa mukashi Nihon no miyako deari, bunka no chūshin ni narimashita.
        Kyoto is the ancient capital of Japan and became [therefore] the cultural center.

[+ **V3**]   Compound Form. Many compound verbs are formed by following the Base 2 of one verb with the Dictionary Form (V3) of another.

aruku *(walk)* + **mawaru** *(turn around)* = **arukimawaru** *(walk around)*

Ex.: **Ichijikan gurai shōtengai o arukimawarimashita.**
     He walked around the marketplace for about one hour.

hanasu *(talk)* + **au** *(fit, be together)* = **hanashiau** *(talk together, discuss)*

Ex.: **Sannin wa hoteru no robii de hanashiaimashita.**
     The three people talked together in the lobby of the hotel.

motsu *(hold)* + **kaeru** *(return)* = **mochikaeru** *(take home, take out)*

Ex.: **O-miyage o katte, Nihon ni mochikaerimashita.**
     He bought souvenirs and took them back to Japan.
     O-mochikaeri desu ka?
     Will this be to go? (as from a store/restaurant)

kaku *(write)* + **naosu** *(fix, repair)* = **kakinaosu** *(rewrite [for correction])*

Ex.: **Kore wa machigai bakari desu kara, kakinaoshite kudasai.**
     This is nothing but errors, so please rewrite it.

-agaru   *do up[wards], be finished.* This ending has limited use, depending on the verb it follows. The verb created is always intransitive (cannot take a direct object).

dekiagaru = *be completed*

Ex.: **Oyu o irete, dekiagarimasu.**
     Add hot water and [the recipe] is completed.

tachiagaru = *stand up*

Ex.: **Sensei wa tachiagatte kokuban ni kakihajimemashita.**
     The teacher stood up and started writing on the blackboard.

-ageru   *do for [someone], do up[wards], finish doing (transitive)*

Ex.: **Oka no ue made oshiagemashō.**
     Let's push it up to the top of the hill.
     Shigoto o shiagereba, kaette mo ii desu.
     When you finish your work, it's okay to go home.

-dasu   *do suddenly, suddenly start doing*

Ex.: **Kotori wa patto tobidashimashita.**
     The little bird suddenly flew off.
     Kodomo wa ie no hō ni hashiridashimashita.
     The child ran off in the direction of the house.

-hajimeru   *begin doing*

Ex.: **Mō osoi desu kara, benkyō shihajimenakute wa ikemasen.**
Since it's late, I have to start studying.

-kata   *way/method of doing, how to.*   Changes the verb into a noun.

Ex.: **Sukiyaki no tsukurikata o oshiete kudasai.**
Please teach me how to make sukiyaki.

Idiomatic: **Shikata ga arimasen.**   *It can't be helped.*

-komu   *do in/into.*   This compound form has limited application, depending on the verb used.

kakikomu = *write in*

Ex.: **Seinengappi o koko ni kakikonde kudasai.**
Please write your birthdate here.

tobikomu = *jump/dive/fly into*

Ex.: **Kotori wa mado garasu ni tobikonde shinde shimaimashita.**
The little bird flew into the window glass and was killed (died).

mōshikomu = *apply [for], make an application*

Ex.: **Kono denwa bangō ni mōshikonde kudasai.**
Please apply to this phone number.

[Masu Form]   A set of verb endings used to end sentences in the Normal-polite level of speech. *(See also Chapter 8, The Masu Form.)*

-masu	present/future tense ("non-past")
-mashita	past tense
-masen	negative present/future tense ("non-past")
-masen deshita	negative past tense
-mashō	inclusive command *(Let's . . .)*
-mashō ka	inclusive query *(Shall we . . .?)*

Ex.: **Maiasa shinbun o yomimasu.**
I read the newspaper every morning.
Yūbe terebi o mimashita ka?
Did you watch TV last night?
Mada tabemasen.   *I won't eat yet.*
O-tomodachi wa kimasen deshita.
Your friend did not come.
Mō kaerimashō.   *Let's go home already.*
Issho ni ikimashō ka?   *Shall we go together?*

-nagara   *while doing*

Ex.: **Shinbun o yominagara, jimusho ni hairimashita.**
He entered the office while reading a newspaper.

-nasai   Abrupt command: *Do it!*

> Ex.:   **Otōsan ni kikinasai yo.**   *Ask your father!*
> **Soto e denasai!**   *Go outside!*

ni iku/kuru   *go/come [somewhere] to do*

> Ex.:   **Depāto e kutsu o kai ni ikimashita.**
> *I went to the department store to buy shoes.*
> **Okāsan to hanashi ni kimashita.**
> *He came to speak with Mother.*

-nikui   *difficult to.* This ending creates a True Adjective.

> Ex.:   **Ano hon wa chotto yominikui desu.**
> *That book is a little hard to read.*
> **Mado wa akinikukatta desu ga, naoshimashita.**
> *The window was hard to open, but I fixed it.*

Idiomatic: **minikui** (from **miru** *[see]*) can mean either "hard to see" or "ugly." **Kikinikui** (from **kiku** *[hear]*) can mean "hard to hear" or "unpleasantly noisy." **Hanashinikui** means "hard to talk to."

-owaru   *finish doing*

> Ex.:   **Tabeowatte, sugu dekakemashita.**
> *He finished eating and immediately went out.*

-sō [desu]   *appear to be about to, look like [+ verb].* This ending creates a Quasi Adjective.

> Ex.:   **Ojiisan wa taoresō desu.**
> *The old man looks like he is going to collapse.*
> **Kodomo wa nakisō na kao o shite imasu.**
> *The child looks like he is going to cry. (Lit. . . . is making a face that looks like . . .)*

-sugiru   *do too much*

> Ex.:   **Yūbe nomisugimashita kara, kyō guai ga warui desu.**
> *I drank too much last night, so today I don't feel well.*

-tagaru   *want to, wish to.* This ending is similar to the Tai Form but adds more intensity of emotion. *(See below for Tai Form.)*

> Ex.:   **Furusato e kaeritagarimasu.**
> *I want to (am eager to/yearn to) return to my hometown.*
> **Kodomo wa aisukuriimu o tabetagarimashita.**
> *The child wanted to (longed to) eat the ice cream.*

-tai [desu]   *want to.* Makes the verb a True Adjective. Also called the **Tai Form** or **Desiderative**. Without **desu**, **-tai** and its conjugated forms

(-takatta, -takunai, -takunakatta) are considered Informal. **Desu** raises
the level to Normal-polite.

Ex.:   **Mō osoi kara, kaeritai desu.**
  Since it's late already, I want to go home.
  Entāteinā ni naritakatta desu.
  I wanted to become an entertainer.
  Shashin o mitai to omoimasu.
  I think I'd like to see the photographs.
  Mada kaeritakunai hito wa, te o agete kudasai.
  *Those people who don't want to go back yet, please raise
  your hands.*

-tsuzukeru   *continue doing*
  Ex.:   **Ichijikan gurai arukitsuzukemashita.**
    He continued walking for about an hour.

-yasui   *easy to.* This ending creates a True Adjective.
  Ex.:   **Fōku wa tsukaiyasui desu.**
    A fork is easy to use.
  Mō chotto yomiyasui hon ga hoshii to omoimasu.
    I think I'd like a book that is a little easier to read.

12. Base 3 Endings

Ex. Verbs	V3
Yodan	
kau	kau
matsu	matsu
shiru	shiru
kaku	kaku
oyogu	oyogu
hanasu	hanasu
shinu	shinu
yomu	yomu
asobu	asobu
Ichidan	
taberu	taberu
miru	miru
Irregular	
kuru	kuru
suru	suru

Base 3 is called the "Dictionary Form" of the verb, since it is the form in which a verb may be found in the dictionary.

V3 is also an Informal Form of the present positive and, in casual situations, can be used instead of V2 + **masu** to end a sentence in the Normal-polite level of speech.

Following is a selection of common V3 endings.

hodo   *to the extent that, so much so that*

Ex.:   **Ojisan wa suteru hodo okane o motte imasu.**
Uncle has 'money to burn.' (. . . to the extent that he could throw it away.)
Kodomo demo dekiru hodo kantan desu.
It's simple enough that even a child can do it.

kagiri   *to the extent that, insofar as, within the limits of*

Ex.:   **Dekiru kagiri, doryoku shimasu.**
I will try to the extent that it is possible.
Watakushi ga shitte iru kagiri, shōjiki na hito desu.
So far as I know, he is an honest person.

kawari [ni]   *instead of, in place of, in exchange for*

Ex.:   **Iku kawari ni denwa o shimashita.** *I phoned instead of going.*
Yō o shite kureru kawari ni Nihongo o oshiete agemasu.
I teach [him] Japanese in exchange for his service to me.

ki ga aru, ki ga suru   *be of a mind to, have a mind to, feel like doing*

Ex.:   **Tenisu o suru ki ga areba, issho ni shimashō ka?**
If you're of a mind to play tennis, shall we play together?

Kyō byōki de, shigoto o suru ki ga shimasen.
Today I am sick and don't feel like working.

ki ni naru   *come to feel like doing*

Ex.:   Sukoshi arukimawaru to benkyō suru ki ni naru deshō.
If you walk around a little, you may come to feel like studying.

koto ga aru   *[ever] do, occasionally do*

Ex.:   Tokidoki o-sushi o taberu koto ga arimasu.
I eat sushi from time to time.
Maitoshi nandoka ryokō o suru koto ga arimasu.
Several times every year I do some traveling.

koto ga dekiru   Potential Form: *be able to do, can do*

Ex.:   Oniisan wa gitā o hiku koto ga dekimasu.
Older brother can play the guitar.
Me ga itakute, miru koto ga dekimasen deshita.
My eyes hurt, and so I wasn't able to see.

Two-word "**suru**" verbs are different in this form: **koto ga** is omitted, and **dekiru** replaces **suru**. If the direct object particle **o** is normally used, it is replaced by **ga**.

Ex.:   Kuruma ga arimasen keredomo, unten dekimasu.
I do not have a car, but I can drive.
Rokuji made ni denwa ga dekimasu ka?
Will you be able to phone by 6:00?

Idiomatic: **benkyō dekimasu/dekimasen** refers to mental state ("I just can't think straight"). To express ability/inability to study (because of lack of time, distractions, etc.), use **benkyō suru koto ga dekimasu/ dekimasen**.

Ex.:   Tsukarete, mō benkyō dekimasen.
I'm tired, and I just can't think any more.
Konban hachiji kara benkyō suru koto ga dekimasu ka?
Can you study from 8:00 tonight?

koto ni naru, yō ni naru   *come about, come to pass, wind up doing, turn out that*

Ex.:   Doyōbi ni mo hataraku koto ni narimashita.
It turns out that I will be working on Saturday, also.
Okāsan ga byōki de, byōin ni iku yō ni narimashita.
Mother was sick, so I wound up going to the hospital.

koto ni suru, yō ni suru   *decide to*

Ex.:   Ashita Tōkyō ni iku koto ni shimashita.
I decided to go to Tokyo tomorrow.

Yahari shachō-san to hanasu yō ni shimashita.
He decided to speak with the company president after all.

made   *until [I] do*

Ex.: **Atarashii no o kau made, kore o tsukatte kudasai.**
Please use this until I buy a new one.
Tokei ga naru made, yasunde kudasai.
Please rest until the clock (alarm) goes off.

made ni   *by the time [I] do*

Ex.: **O-kyakusan ga kuru made ni, dekiagaru to omoimasu.**
I think it will be finished by the time the guests come.

mae [ni]   *before doing*

Ex.: **Kaeru mae ni o-mise ni yotte kudasai.**
Please go by the store before coming home.
Kochira ni kuru mae ni, Hawai ni sunde imashita.
I was living in Hawaii before coming here.

mono   *thing.* Creates a relative clause that may refer to a thing, a person, an obligation, or a reason to do something; or it may be used as an emphatic suggestion or instruction.

Ex.: **Taberu mono wa arimasen ka?** *Don't you have anything to eat?*
O-toshiyori wa, yukkuri yasumu mono desu.
[You] being older, you should get plenty of rest.

na   Abrupt or emphatic negative command: *Don't do it!*

Ex.: **Sonna koto o iu na!** *Don't say such things!*
Wasureru na! *Don't forget!*

tame [ni]   *in order to, for the sake of*

Ex.: **Kodomo ga wakaru tame ni hakkiri to setsumei shite kudasai.**
In order for the children to understand, please explain clearly.
Buchō-san to hanasu tame ni hayaku kimashita.
I came early in order to speak with the department head.

With the Progressive Form, this ending means "because" or "since."

Ex.: **Oniisan ga benkyō shite iru tame, soto de asonde kudasai.**
Since your older brother is studying, please play outside.

to   *if [I] do*

Ex.: **Kyōto ni yoru to, tomodachi ni awanakute wa narimasen.**
If you stop by Kyoto, you must see my friend.
Sō suru to, okāsan ga yorokobu deshō.
If you do that, your mom will probably be glad.

tochū [desu]   *be en route/on the way.* Used with verbs of motion.

Ex.: **Ima kaisha e iku tochū desu.** *I am en route to the company now.*

Gakkō e iku tochū de tomodachi ni aimashita.
I met a friend on my way to school.

tokoro [desu]   *be about to*

Ex.: **Ima chotto dekakeru tokoro desu.** *We are about to go out now.*

With the Progressive Form, this ending means "be in the process of."

Ex.: **Ima renshū shite iru tokoro desu.**
I am in the process of practicing now.

Idiomatic: **Watakushi no shitte iru tokoro de wa . . .**
As far as I know . . .

to shitara, to sureba, to suru to   Emphatic Conditional: *if [I] were to,*
if [I] did, if [I] do

Ex.: **Kuruma o kau to shitara, donna mono ga ii ka shira?**
If we were to buy a car, what kind would be best?
O-tomodachi ga kuru to sureba, gogatsu deshō.
If your friend does come, it will probably be in May.
Moshi Hawai ni tomaru to suru to, hitoban dake deshō.
If we do stop in Hawaii, it will probably be only one night.

to shite mo   *even if*

Ex.: **Okāsan ni kiku to shite mo, otōsan ga sansei shinai to omoimasu.**
Even if we ask Mother, I think Father will not approve.

tsumori [desu]   *intend to*

Ex.: **Ashita densha de iku tsumori desu.**
I intend to go by train tomorrow.

yō ni   *in order to*

Ex.: **Asu dekakerareru yō ni junbi shite imasu.**
I am preparing to be able to depart tomorrow.
Jōzu ni dekiru yō ni mainichi renshū shimasu.
I practice every day in order to become skillful.

yō ni naru, yō ni suru   *(See* **koto ni naru, koto ni suru.***)*

yotei [desu]   *plan to*

Ex.: **Asu tenisu o suru yotei desu.** *I plan to play tennis tomorrow.*

13. Base 4 Endings

Ex. Verbs	V4
Yodan	
kau	kae-
matsu	mate-
shiru	shire-
kaku	kake-
oyogu	oyoge-
hanasu	hanase-
shinu	shine-
yomu	yome-
asobu	asobe-
Ichidan	
taberu	tabere-
miru	mire-
Irregular	
kuru	kure-
	kore-
suru	sure-

Base 4 is sometimes called the "Conditional Base." There are relatively few endings that require Base 4; most of them have a conditional aspect.

Note that all verbs in Base 4 end in the vowel **e**. Also, the verb **kuru** has two forms listed for Base 4; the verb ending determines which of the two forms is required.

Following is a selection of common V4 endings.

[No ending]   Abrupt command: *do it!*

Ex.: **Hanase!** *Let go!*
Damare! *Shut up!*
Yame! *Quit it!*

Kuru in this form is **koi**. In two-word verbs **suru** becomes **seyo** (eg, **benkyō seyo**); otherwise, **suru** may be replaced by the more colloquial **yaru** (**yare**).

-ba   Conditional: *if/when [I] do.* (**Kuru** becomes **kureba**.)

Ex.: **Isogeba, maniaimasu.** *If we hurry, we'll be on time.*
Aisukuriimu wa sukoshi dake tabereba ii desu.
It's okay if you eat just a little ice cream.

Desu: naraba

Ex.: **Ano hito naraba issho ni itte mo ii desu.**
If it's him (that person), it's okay to go along.

-ba yokatta [desu]   *it would be better if [I] had done.* (**Kuru: kureba . . .**)

Ex.: **Hayaku tabereba yokatta desu.**
It would be better if I had eaten early.

-ru Potential: *able to, can.* This ending is used only with Yodan verbs and **kuru** in Base 4. (For Ichidan verbs the Potential ending is **V1** + **rareru**; **suru** becomes **dekiru** in the Potential form.) This ending creates a new verb that is classified as Ichidan no matter what the original verb was.

Ex.: **Kono pen de kakemasen.** *I can't write with this pen.*
Nihongo wa yomemasu ka? *Can you read Japanese?*
Ashita koremasen ka? *Can't you come tomorrow?*

Exceptional: **miru** *(see)* – **mieru** *(be visible)*; **kiku** *(hear)* – **kikoeru** *(be audible)*

Ex.: **Mukō no fune ga miemasu ka?**
Can you see the ship over yonder? (Lit. Is the ship over yonder visible?)
Shizuka ni natte, okashii oto ga kikoemashita.
It became quiet and I was able to hear the strange noise. (Lit. . . . noise was audible.)

14. Base 5 Endings

Ex. Verbs	V5
Yodan	
kau	ka̅o̅
matsu	mato̅
shiru	shiro̅
kaku	kako̅
oyogu	oyogo̅
hanasu	hanaso̅
shinu	shino̅
yomu	yomo̅
asobu	asobo̅
Ichidan	
taberu	tabeyo̅
miru	miyo̅
Irregular	
kuru	koyo̅
suru	shiyo̅

Base 5 is sometimes called the "Conjectural Base." There are relatively few endings that require Base 5.

Note that all verbs end in a long **o** in this base.

Following is a selection of common V5 endings.

[No ending] Informal inclusive command: *Let's . . . (Cf. V2 + mashō.)* Used in casual situations.

Ex.: **Mō osoi kara, kaerō.** *It's late already, so let's go home. (Casual)*
Ashita shiken desu kara, benkyō shiyō yo. *(Casual)*
Tomorrow is the test, so let's study!

ka Informal inclusive query: *Shall we . . . ? (Cf. V2 + mashō ka.)* Used in casual situations.

Ex.: **Ichiji-han ni hajimeyō ka?** *Shall we start at 1:30? (Casual)*
Asu mata koyō ka? *Shall we come again tomorrow? (Casual)*

to omou *I think I will*

Ex.: **Kyō tomodachi no ie ni ikō to omoimasu.**
I think I will go to my friend's house today.
Ashita mata koyō to omotte imasu.
I am thinking I will [probably] come again tomorrow.

to suru *be about to.* Most often used in the Progressive Form **to shite iru.**

Ex.: **Sensei wa jugyō o hajimeyō to shite imasu.**
The teacher is about to start the lesson.
Keisatsu ni denwa shiyō to shite imasu.
He is about to phone the police.

15. Base 6 (TE-form) Endings

Ex. Verbs	Vte
Yodan	
kau	katte
matsu	matte
shiru	shitte
kaku	kaite
oyogu	oyoide
hanasu	hanashite
shinu	shinde
yomu	yonde
asobu	asonde
Ichidan	
taberu	tabete
miru	mite
Irregular	
kuru	kite
suru	shite

Base 6 is more often referred to as the TE-form or Vte. Use of Vte indicates that another verb will follow, either immediately or later in the sentence.

Iku *(go)* is irregular in the TE-form: **itte**.

The TE-form of **desu** is **de**.

Vte has wide usage; following is a selection of common Vte endings.

[**Verbs in series**]   Continuation Form: Indicates a series of actions given more or less in sequence. Sometimes there is a mild cause/effect implication. "And," "and then," or "and so" may be used in translation. Final verb in the series is in whatever form it would take if there were no other verbs. All verbs in the series take the tense (past or present) of the final verb.

Ex.:   **Uchi e kaette, shokuji o shimashita.**
   I returned home and [then] had dinner.
   Tabete kimashita. *I ate and [then] came.*
   Tabako o sutte, byōki ni narimashita.
   He smoked a cigarette and [so] he got sick.

Desu: With **desu** sequence is irrelevant. Mild cause/effect implication is common.

Ex.:   **Ano hito wa Nihonjin de, Eigo ga dekimasen.**
   That person is Japanese and can't [speak] English.

ageru, yaru   *do for [someone other than the speaker]*. **Yaru** is more casual. **Ageru** is preferred when talking to the person for whom the action is taken.

Ex.:   **Chizu o kaite agemashō ka?** *Shall I draw you a map?*

> Tomodachi ni misete yarō to omoimasu.
> *I think I will show it to my friend.*

aru   *has been done*

Ex.:   **Tegami wa mō kaite arimasu.**
        The letters have already been written.
        Denki wa mō tsukete arimashita.
        The lights had already been turned on.

hoshii [desu]   *want [someone] to.* Hoshii is a True Adjective.

Ex.:   **Okāsan ni katte hoshii desu.** *I want Mother to buy it.*
        Yasai o tabete hoshikatta desu.
        I wanted you to eat the vegetables.

iku   *do and [then] go, do before going*

Ex.:   **Sensei to hanashite ikimashō.**
        Let's talk with the teacher and [then] go.

Idiomatic: **motte iku** *(take and go, take [with you])*. The item taken must be a thing, not a person.

Ex.:   **Kono hon o motte ikimasu.**
        I will take this book [with me].

iru   Progressive Form: *be doing.* (action in progress)

Ex.:   **Otōsan wa ima shinbun o yonde imasu.**
        Father is reading the newspaper now.

Exception: Verbs of motion and some other verbs with this ending take on a perfective form ("has done," "had done," etc.). *(See V3 + tochū for motion in progress.)*

Ex.:   **Tanaka-san wa ima Hawai e itte imasu.**
        Tanaka has gone to Hawaii.
        Yoji ni buchō-san wa mō ie ni kaette imashita.
        At 4:00 the department head had already returned home.

itadaku, morau   *have [someone] do.* The person of whom the action is required is followed by **ni**. When talking to that person, **itadaku** is preferred, since **morau** is somewhat more casual.

Ex.:   **Ashita sensei ni oshiete itadakimasu.**
        I will have the teacher tell (teach) me tomorrow.
        Konban denwa o shite itadakemasu ka?
        Can I have you telephone tonight?
        Shōnen wa otona no tomodachi ni biiru o katte moraimashita.
        The young boys had their adult friend buy the beer.

kara   *after doing*

> Ex.: **Tabete kara, shukudai o suru yotei desu.**
> *I plan to do homework after I eat.*
> **Denwa o shite kara, ima ni kite kudasai.**
> *After phoning, please come into the living room.*

kudasai   Polite request: *Please do.* Adding **-masu ka** or **-masen ka** raises
the level of politeness.

> Ex.: **Chotto matte kudasai.** *Please wait a moment.*
> **Kore o mite kudasaimasu ka?** *Will you please look at this?*
> **Ashita made ni denwa o shite kudasaimasen ka?**
> *Won't you please phone by tomorrow?*

kuru   *do and come [back], do before coming*

> Ex.: **Tabete kimashita.**
> *I ate before I came. (Lit. I ate and [then] came.)*
> **Buchō-san to chotto hanashite kimasu.**
> *I will talk with the department head for a moment and come
> back.*

Idiomatic:

motte kuru   *bring* (referring to things, not people)

> Ex.: **Kasa o motte kimasen deshita.** *I didn't bring an umbrella.*

itte kuru   *be [right] back (Lit. go and come)*

> Ex.: **Sumimasen, chotto itte kimasu.** *Excuse me, I'll be right back.*

wasurete kuru   *forget to bring (Lit. forget and come)*

> Ex.: **Kyōkasho o wasurete kimashita.**
> *I forgot to bring my textbooks.*

miru   *do and see, try doing*

> Ex.: **Oishii desu kara, tabete mite kudasai.**
> *It's delicious, [so] eat it and see.*
> **Ayashii oto ga kikoeta kara, heya ni haitte mimashita.**
> *I heard a suspicious noise, so I went into the room to see
> (check it out).*

mo   *even if [I] do*

> Ex.: **Tomodachi ga kite mo, dekakete wa ikemasen.**
> *Even if your friend comes, you are not allowed to go out.*
> **Hashitte mo, maniawanai to omoimasu.**
> *Even if we run, I think we won't make it in time.*

mo ii [desu]   *It's okay to.* (Variations: **mo daijōbu desu, mo kamaimasen.**)

   Ex.: **Hayaku kaette mo ii desu ka?**
       Is it okay if I go home early?
       Sukoshi tabete mo ii desu.
       It's okay to eat a little bit.

morau   *(See* **itadaku.***)*

oku   *do for a later purpose, do and set aside, do in advance, go ahead and do*

   Ex.: **Shuppatsu wa ashita desu kara, kyō nizukuri o shite okimasu.**
       Since our departure is tomorrow, I will pack today.
       Ashita tesuto desu kara, benkyō shite okimashō.
       Tomorrow [there] is a test, so let's go ahead and study.

   do and leave it as is/leave it in other hands

   Ex.: **Taisetsu desu kara, kachō-san ni itte okimasu.**
       It's important, so I will tell the section chief and leave it in his hands.

shimau   *do completely/irrevocably/irretrievably*

   Ex.: **Kangaenakute, itte shimaimashita.**
       Without thinking, I said it right out.
       Wasurete shimaimashita. *I completely forgot.*
       Dokoka de saifu o nakushite shimaimashita.
       Somewhere I [irretrievably] lost my wallet.

wa ikemasen, wa dame desu   *It's not okay to, [I] had better not/should not*

   Ex.: **Koko de tabako o sutte wa ikemasen.**
       It's not okay to smoke here.
       Toshokan no naka de ōgoe de hanashite wa dame desu.
       It's not okay to talk out loud in the library.

yaru   *(See* **ageru.***)*

16. Base 7 (TA-form) Endings

Ex. Verbs	Vta
Yodan	
kau	katta
matsu	matta
shiru	shitta
kaku	kaita
oyogu	oyoida
hanasu	hanashita
shinu	shinda
yomu	yonda
asobu	asonda
Ichidan	
taberu	tabeta
miru	mita
Irregular	
kuru	kita
suru	shita

Base 7 (TA-form or Vta) is also called the "Plain Past" or "Informal Past" because it is used in Casual speech to indicate past tense.

Vta has the same form as Vte, except for the final vowel.

Iku *(go)* is irregular in the TA-form: **itta.**

The TA-form of **desu** is **datta. Deatta** is also possible.

Following is a selection of Vta endings.

[No ending]   Informal past tense: *did. (Cf. V2 + mashita.)*

> Ex.: **Sukoshi yasunda.** *I rested a little. (Casual)*

ato   *after having done, after doing*

> Ex.: **Tabeta ato, dekakemashita.** *After eating, I went out.*
> **Owatta ato, denwa o shimasu.**
> *I will telephone after I have finished.*

bakari [desu]   *have just done*

> Ex.: **Ima tabeta bakari desu.** *I have just finished eating.*
> **Suzuki-san ga tsuita bakari da to omoimasu.**
> *I think Mr. Suzuki has just arrived.*

koto ga aru   *have [ever] done, have had the experience of doing*

> Ex.: **Yōroppa ni itta koto ga arimasu ka?**
> *Have you ever been (gone) to Europe?*
> **Sashimi o tabeta koto ga arimasen.** *I have never eaten raw fish.*

ra   *If [I] do/did*

> Ex.: **O-tomodachi ga ima denwa o shitara, dō shimasu ka?**
> *What would you do if your friend phoned now?*

Okane ga nakunattara, komarimasu.
I would be in trouble if my money ran out.

When the main verb is past tense, this ending takes the meaning "when [I] did."

Ex.: **Sensei ni kiitara, hakkiri to wakarimashita.**
When I asked the teacher, I understood clearly.

ri   Nonsequential series of verbs. The final verb is usually followed by some form of **suru**. The implication is that other things than those stated may take place or have taken place. Tense (past or present) of all verbs in the series is determined by the final verb.

Ex.: **Gakkō ga owatte kara, tegami o kaitari, ongaku o kiitari shimasu.**
After school is over, I write letters, listen to music, and things like that (in no particular order).

tame [ni]   *because [I] did*

Ex.: **Sensei ga itta tame, shinjimashita.**
Because the teacher said it, I believed it.
Tegami o uketa tame ni, denwa o shimashita.
I phoned because I received [your] letter.
Kibun ga warui desu ga, yoku nenakatta tame desu.
I don't feel well, but it's because I didn't sleep well.

tokoro [desu]   *just did, [be at] the point of having done*

Ex.: **Ima shokuji ga owatta tokoro desu.**
I just now finished dinner. (Lit. Dinner is now at the point of having been finished.)

17. The Informal Form

The term "Informal Form" refers to certain verb and adjective forms that may replace the Normal-polite (**desu-masu**) endings in specific situations. Informal Forms are sometimes called "Abrupt" or "Plain" forms. They have both social and grammatical applications:

- **In casual social situations,** such as when talking with family or close friends, the Informal Form is preferred over Normal-polite.

- The Informal is also broadly used **in impersonal speech,** such as broadcast news, announcements, etc. The difference between these situations and casual conversations shows up clearly in the selection of polite verbs and other vocabulary and expressions to suit the more formal circumstances.

- **Grammatical applications** include certain endings that are commonly used with Informal forms of verbs or adjectives. A selection of such endings is presented in Chapter 18.

Informal of Verbs

Informal Verb Forms	Corresponding Normal-polite *(Masu Form)*
V3	V2 + **masu** (present/future tense ["non-past"])
Vta	V2 + **mashita** (past tense)
V1 + **nai**	V2 + **masen** (negative present/future ["non-past"])
V1 + **nakatta**	V2 + **masen deshita** (negative past)
V5	V2 + **mashō** (inclusive command)

Example Verb: **yomu** *(to read)*

Informal Form	Normal-polite	English Equivalent
yo**mu**	yomi**masu**	*read/reads*
yo**nda**	yomi**mashita**	*read/did read*
yo**manai**	yomi**masen**	*do not/does not read*
yo**manakatta**	yomi**masen deshita**	*did not read*
yo**mō**	yomi**mashō**	*Let's read.*

Verb endings that employ auxiliary verbs or create new verbs have the same Informal/Normal-polite relationship; for example:

PROGRESSIVE FORM

Informal Form	Normal-polite	English Equivalent
yonde iru	yonde imasu	*is/are reading*
yonde ita	yonde imashita	*was/were reading*
yonde inai	yonde imasen	*is/are not reading*
yonde inakatta	yonde imasen deshita	*was/were not reading*

(Inclusive command forms **yonde iyō/yonde imashō** are seldom used.)

CAUSATIVE FORM

yomaseru	yomasemasu	*cause to read*
yomaseta	yomasemashita	*caused to read*
yomasenai	yomasemasen	*does not cause to read*
yomasenakatta	yomasemasen deshita	*did not cause to read*

(Inclusive command forms **yomaseyō/yomasemashō** are seldom used.)

Informal of DESU

Informal Form	Normal-polite	English Equivalent
da/dearu*	desu	*is/are*
datta/deatta*	deshita	*was/were*
dewanai	dewa arimasen	*is not/are not*
dewanakatta	dewa arimasen deshita	*was not/were not*
darō/dearō*	deshō	*probably/possibly is*

*Even though the forms **dearu, deatta,** and **dearō** are grammatically Informal, in many cases their use adds a more formal flavor to the sentence than either the shorter Informal forms or the Normal-polite. In most cases where a verb ending calls for an Informal form, either of the Informal choices can be used; in a few cases, however, one is preferred over the other.

Informal of ARU

The Informal Form of **aru** *(be located; have)* is irregular in the negative only.

Informal Form	Normal-polite	English Equivalent
aru	arimasu	*is/are located*
atta	arimashita	*was/were located*
nai	arimasen	*is not/are not located*
nakatta	arimasen deshita	*was not/were not located*

(Inclusive command forms for this verb are not applicable.)

Informal of Adjectives

The Informal Form of a **True Adjective** is simply the adjective (even in conjugated forms) **without** <u>desu</u>, as it appears when placed immediately before a noun.

Informal: **Kinō atsukatta, ne.** *(Casual)*
Norm-pol: **Kinō atsukatta desu, ne.**
It was hot yesterday, wasn't it?

This is true also of verb endings that change the verb to a True Adjective form, such as **[V1 +] nai**, **[V2 +] tai**, **[V2 +] nikui**, etc.

Informal: **Ashita ikanai.** *(Casual)*
Norm-pol: **Ashita ikanai desu.** / **Ashita ikimasen.**
I'm not going tomorrow.

Informal: **Mada kaeritakunakatta.** *(Casual)*
Norm-pol: **Mada kaeritakunakatta desu.**
I didn't want to go home yet.

Informal: **Kanji wa yominikui, ne.** *(Casual)*
Norm-pol: **Kanji wa yominikui desu, ne.**
Kanji is hard to read, isn't it?

For **Quasi** and **Noun + NO Adjectives**, the Informal of **desu** is usually used.

Informal: **Kesa byōki datta.** *(Casual)*
Norm-pol: **Kesa byōki deshita.**
I was sick this morning.

However, some endings require a particle between the Quasi or Noun + NO Adjective and the ending. This is particularly true if the ending is or begins with a noun form, such as **hazu, aida, baai, hō** etc.

Ex.: **Toshokan wa shizuka na hazu desu.**
The library is supposed to be quiet.
Otōto wa byōki no aida zutto kurushimimashita.
Younger brother suffered continually while he was sick.

18. Informal Endings

Following is a selection of common endings used with Informal verb and adjective forms in the Normal-polite level of speech. Note that the Informal inclusive command (V5) is not used with these endings.

aida   *while, during.*

Ex.: **Otōsan ga nete iru aida, shizuka ni shite kudasai.**
Please be quiet while your father is sleeping.
Sensei dearu aida, kono heya o jimushitsu ni shimasu.
While I am a teacher, I will make this room my office.

Idiomatic: **nagai aida** = *[for] a long time*
mijikai aida = *[for] a short while*

Ex.: **Nagai aida hanashiaimashita.**   *We talked together for a long time.*

baai   *whenever, in the case of*

Ex.: **Issho ni iku baai, itsumo saki ni denwa shimasu.**
Whenever we go together, I always telephone ahead of time.
Shokuryō ga yasui baai, takusan kaimasu.
Whenever food is inexpensive, I buy a lot.
Sensei dearu baai, kyūryō ga tarinai to omoimasu.
In the case of [being] a teacher, I think the pay is insufficient.

dake   *only, just, simply*

Ex.: **Miru dake desu.**   *I'm just looking.*
Ano kuruma wa hayakunakute, kirei dake desu.
That car is not fast, it's only pretty.

Idiomatic: **dekiru dake** = *as [much as] possible, insofar as possible, if possible*

Ex.: **Dekiru dake, rokuji made ni owatte hoshii desu.**
If possible, I want you to finish by 6:00.

deshō   *probably/likely*

Ex.: **Ashita ame ga furu deshō.**
It will probably rain tomorrow.
Mō kaetta deshō.   *He probably went home already.*
Kamawanai deshō.   *It probably won't matter.*
Suzuki-san no kuruma wa chiisai deshō.
Suzuki's car is probably small.

Desu is replaced by **deshō**.

Ex.: **Asoko no hito wa sensei deshō.**
The person over there is probably the teacher.

hazu [desu]   *is supposed/expected to, should/ought to*

Ex.: **O-kyakusan wa nanji ni kuru hazu desu ka?**
What time is your guest supposed to come?
Yūbe shuppatsu shita hazu desu.
They were supposed to depart at 9:00 last night. (Lit. They are supposed to have departed . . .)
Ashita made kaette konai hazu desu.*
He is not supposed to come home until tomorrow.
Supeingo wa kantan na hazu desu.
The Spanish language is supposed to be simple.

*Another way of saying "is not supposed to" is **hazu wa nai** [desu] or **hazu wa arimasen**.

Ex.: **Mada basu ga kuru hazu wa nai desu.**
The bus is not supposed to come yet.
Kono hana wa shiroi hazu wa arimasen.
These flowers shouldn't be white.

hō ga ii [desu]   *had better, it is better/best to.* Indicates a preference for one action or characteristic over other possible choices. *(See also Chapter 28, Comparisons.)*

Ex.: **Mainichi benkyō suru hō ga ii desu.**   *It is best to study every day.*
Hayaku kaetta hō ga ii desu.   *You had better go home early.*
Futsū wa yasui hō ga ii desu, ne.
Usually cheap[er] is better, isn't it?
Kirei na hō ga ii to omoimasu.   *I think it is better if it is clean.*
Bin wa kara no hō ga ii deshō.
It's probably better if the bottle is empty.

ka dō ka   *whether or not.* Usually used with positive verbs, past or present.

Ex .: **Denwa ga dekita ka dō ka iimasen deshita.**
He didn't say whether or not he was able to phone.
Takai ka dō ka wakaranai desu.
I don't know if it's expensive or not.
Sensei dearu ka dō ka, kamawanai to omoimasu.
I think it doesn't matter whether he is a teacher or not.

ka mo shirenai/shiremasen   *may/may not [for all one knows]* . The Informal **shirenai** is often used even in Normal-polite speech.

Ex.: **Kyō wa ame desu ga, ashita wa hareru ka mo shirenai.**
It's raining today, but it may clear up tomorrow, for all we know.

Mō kaetta ka mo shiremasen.
He may have gone home already, for all I know.
Mada wakaranai keredomo, yasui ka mo shiremasen.
I don't know yet, but it might be cheap.
Mae wa sensei datta ka mo shirenai.
He might have been a teacher before.

ka na/ka shira   *I wonder if*

Ex.: **Okusan mo kuru ka shira.**
I wonder if his wife will come, too.
Mō owatta ka na. *I wonder if it's over yet.*
O-tomodachi mo ikitai ka na.
I wonder if your friend wants to come, too.
Ano hito wa sensei datta ka shira.
I wonder if he was a teacher.

koto   Makes verb into a noun. Literally means "thing," referring to an intangible thing, concept or fact. *(See also Chapter 31, Relative Clauses.)*

Ex.: **Utau koto ga suki desu.** *I like to sing.*
Shachō-san ga itta koto o oboete imasu ka?
Do you remember what the company president said?
Kodomo-tachi mo ikitakatta koto o wasuremashita.
I forgot [the fact] that the children also wanted to go.

mitai/rashii [desu]   *appear to, look like [+ verb]*

Ex.: **Mō owatta rashii desu.** *It looks like it's finished already.*
Sensei ga konai rashii desu. *It looks like the teacher isn't coming.*
Yahari suki dewanakatta mitai desu.
It looks like he didn't like it after all.

nara   *if*

Ex.: **Hayaku okiru nara, kodomo mo okoshite kudasai.**
If you wake up early, wake up the children also.
Takai nara, kaenai to omoimasu.
If it's expensive, I think I can't buy it.

A True Adjective may be followed by **no** before **nara**.

Ex.: **Yasui no nara, futatsu katte kudasai.**
If it's cheap, please buy two.

Desu is replaced by **nara**.

Ex.: **Kanojo no hon nara, kaeshimasu.**
If it is her book, I will return it.

ni chigai nai/arimasen   *definitely/without doubt.* Although **[chigai] nai** is an Informal form, it is acceptable in Normal-polite speech. Often the phrase **to omoimasu** is added to soften the sentence. *(See Chapter 19, Basic Principles: Softening a Sentence.)*

Ex.: **Sonna ni takusan taberu to byōki ni naru ni chigai arimasen.**
  If you eat that much, you will surely get sick.
  Okureta ni chigai nai.   *He undoubtedly was late.*
  Ashita kuru ni chigai nai to omoimasu.
  I think he will definitely come tomorrow.
  Ano hito wa gaijin dearu ni chigai nai to omoimasu.
  I think that person is undoubtedly a foreigner.

no   Indefinite pronoun: *the thing/the one.* This is similar to **koto** in that it makes a verb into a noun; the 'thing' that **no** refers to may or may not be tangible.

Ex.: **Iroiro na kangaekata ga arimasu ga, Tanaka-san ga setsumei shita no wa mottomo omoshiroi to omoimasu.**
  There are various ways of thinking, but I think the most interesting is the one that Tanaka has explained.
  A: Dochira ga suki desu ka?
  B: Ichiban chiisai no ga kirei da to omoimasu.
  A: Which one do you like?
  B: I think the smallest one is prettiest.

Quasi Adjectives are followed by **na** before **no**.

Ex.: **Kodomo wa minna kawaii desu ga, ichiban kirei na no wa ano ko desu.**
  All the children are cute, but the prettiest one is that child.

no [desu]   Comparable to "It is that . . .," this ending is a frequent alternative to the Masu Form and raises the politeness of the Informal Form somewhat by softening the tone of the sentence. In Casual speech it is often contracted to **n'desu** or just **no**.

Ex.: **Onēsan mo iku no desu.**
  [It is that] older sister will go, too.
  Shokuji wa mō owattan' desu.   *(Casual)*
  Dinner is already over.
  Ano ko wa zenzen benkyō shinai no.   *(Casual)*
  That kid doesn't study at all.
  Kore wa yasui no desu, ne.
  This is cheap, isn't it?

Quasi and Noun + NO Adjectives, as well as other nouns, are followed by **na** before **no desu**. In Casual speech, this is sometimes contracted to **nan' desu** or just **na no**.

Ex.: **Ano ko wa totemo kirei na no desu, ne.**
  That child is very pretty, isn't she?

Yukiko wa kyō byōki na no. *(Casual)*
Yukiko is sick today.

no ni   *although/even though/despite the fact*

Ex.: **Isshōkenmei ni benkyō shita no ni, shiken wa dame ni natte shimaimashita.**
Although he studied diligently, the test turned out badly.
Zuibun takai no ni, katte shimaimashita.
I bought it despite the fact that it is really expensive.
Otona dearu no ni, hontō ni kodomo mitai desu.
Even though he is an adult, he really seems like a child.

sō desu   *I hear/heard that*

Ex.: **Raishū Hawai ni iku sō desu.**
I hear that you are going to Hawaii next week.
Tanaka-san ga kekkon shita sō desu.
I heard that Tanaka got married.
Ano ike wa totemo fukai sō desu.
I hear that that pond is very deep.
O-tomodachi wa kachō da sō desu. (or dearu sō desu.)
I hear that your friend is a section chief.

to   Conditional: *If/when.* Used primarily with non-past forms.

Ex.: **Roppongi e iku to ii resutoran ga takusan arimasu.**
If/when you go to Roppongi, there are lots of good restaurants.
Denwa o shinai to, komarimasu.
If you don't phone, I will be in a bind.
Furui to, suteru hō ga ii desu.
If it's old, it's better to throw it away.
Sensei da to, taihen desu. (or Sensei dearu to . . .)
If he's a teacher, that's awful.

to [+ Verb]   Reported speech (indirect quotation)

Ex.: **Okāsan wa kodomo ga tabenakatta to iimashita.**
Mother said the children did not eat.
Ashita kuru to tegami ni kakimashita.
He wrote in a letter that he will come tomorrow.
Atarashii kuruma ga hayai to itta no desu.
He said his new car is fast.
Sensei da (or dearu) to iimashita ka?
Did he say he is a teacher?

toki   *when, time when. (See also Chapter 31, Relative Clauses.)*

Ex.: **Hawai ni tomaru toki, itsumo tomodachi ni denwa o shimasu.**
When I stop in Hawaii, I always telephone my friend.

Yōroppa de ryokō shite ita toki, ban o karite ikimashita.
When we were traveling in Europe, we rented a van [and went around].

Okane ga nai toki, o-bentō o motte ikimasu.
When I don't have any money, I take a box lunch.

to omou   *[I] think that*

Ex.: **Ashita kau to omoimasu.** *I think he will buy it tomorrow.*
Kondo wa ikanai to omoimasu. *I think I won't go this time.*
Chotto takai to omoimasen ka?
Don't you think it is a little expensive?
Oisha-san no nōto da (or **dearu**) **to omoimasu.**
I think it is the doctor's notebook.

uchi ni   *while, during.* Usually used after a present-tense verb, negative or positive. Often used after a Progressive Form.

Ex.: **Tabete iru uchi ni onaka ga itakunarimashita.**
My stomach started hurting while I was eating.
Shiranai uchi ni, inu ga heya ni haitte kimashita.
While I was unaware, the dog came into the room.

wake desu   *It is that, It is because*

Ex.: **Maiasa hayaku okiru wake desu.**
It is that he gets up early every morning.
Densha ga hijō ni konde ita wake de, osokunarimashita.
I was late because the trains were extremely crowded.
Konshū totemo isogashii wake desu.
It is because I am very busy this week.
Kōen ga shizuka na wake desu. *It is that the park is quiet.*

Desu is sometimes replaced by **to iu** before **wake**.

Ex.: **Sensei to iu wake desu, ne.** *It is that he is a teacher, right?*

yō   *appear to, look like [+ verb].* This creates a Quasi Adjective. In front of a noun, **yō** may be translated "kind of," "sort of" or "type of."

Ex.: **Suzuki-san ga konban shuppatsu suru yō desu.**
It looks like Suzuki will depart this evening.
Kore wa hajime ni jimusho datta yō desu.
It looks like this was an office in the beginning.
Obāsan wa dare ni mo yorokonde sewa o suru yō na hito desu.
Grandmother is the kind of person who gladly gives service to anyone.

Part Two:
Essentials of Grammar

19. Basic Principles

Sentence Order

TOPIC/SUBJECT - OBJECT - VERB

TOPIC/SUBJECT

The topic of the Japanese sentence is simply what the rest of the sentence is talking about or referring to, and it may or may not have an obvious grammatical relationship to the rest of the sentence. In most Japanese sentences the topic and the grammatical subject are the same. In cases where they differ, the topic will normally come first, with the subject placed closer to the verb. *(See Chapter 21, Particles: WA, for more on the topic.)*

VERB

The verb always comes at the end of the sentence. The only things that may legitimately follow the verb are a particle, such as **ka** (question) or **yo** (emphasis); a tag question, such as **ne** or **deshō**; or another verb or clause. The remainder of the sentence, although not totally arbitrary, is very flexible.

OBJECT

This refers to what is usually called the "predicate" in Western languages and, for our purposes, includes essentially anything else in the sentence. The arrangement of individual phrases within the sentence is very flexible, as long as the verb is kept at the end.

Time references usually are placed either immediately before the topic or immediately after it. Location references usually come just after the topic. It is possible to put a time or location reference just in front of the verb to add emphasis or to accommodate some other requirement of the sentence.

Descriptive words/phrases come before the word they modify.

In a sentence that has one or more dependent clauses, the main clause will always come last, no matter what the order may be in the English sentence.

> Ex.: **Osokunarimashita kara, kaerimashita.**
> *I went home because it got late.*
> **Ōsaka ni iku to shitara, hitori de ikimasu ka?**
> *If you do go to Osaka, will you go alone?*

QUESTIONS

Word order for questions is the same as for statements, but with the particle **ka** following the verb.

Ex.: **Doko kara kimashita ka?**
 Where do (did) you come from?
 Ōsaka kara kimashita.
 I come (came) from Osaka.

NEGATIVE QUESTIONS

A question with a negative verb is often treated as if it were a "true-false" question; for example, the response to **Kōhii o nomimasen ka?** *(Won't you have some coffee?)* may be **Hai, nomimasen** *(Yes, I won't)* or **Iie, nomimasu** *(No, I will)*, since it is literally asking "Will you *not* have some coffee?"

Sometimes the Japanese will answer a negative question according to the sense of the expected answer, but the usual expectation of a negative question is as shown above. A safe way of answering is to eliminate **hai** or **iie** and respond with a negative or positive verb or some other appropriate phrase.

TAG QUESTIONS

Tag questions are short questions "tagged" onto the end of a sentence, asking for confirmation of what was stated in the sentence. In English tag questions must agree with the subject and verb of the statement ("He said so, *didn't he?*"). Japanese **tag questions** do not require agreement, comparable to adding "Right?" after an English sentence.

The words **ne** and **deshō** are the two most common Japanese tag questions, and they are essentially interchangeable, with one caution: **ne** is simply added after the verb, no matter what that verb is; **deshō** replaces **desu** but is added after any other verb.

Ex.: **Suzuki-san wa mō kaerimashita, ne?**
 Suzuki-san wa mō kaerimashita, deshō?
 Suzuki went home already, didn't he?
 Ashita wa Suiyōbi desu, ne?
 Ashita wa Suiyōbi, deshō?
 Tomorrow is Wednesday, isn't it?

Articles & "It"

There are no articles ("a," "an," "the") in Japanese. In translation they should be simply omitted, although it is acceptable to use **sono** (or **kono** or **ano**) to refer to a specific item or **aru** *(a certain [noun])* to refer to a non-specific item; however, overuse of these words may sound foreign.

There is no word in Japanese corresponding to "it." **Kore/sore/are** *(this/ that/that over there)* can be used, but these substitutions are not neccessary and will sound foreign if used too often.

Nouns & Pronouns

NOUNS

Japanese nouns do not change form for case (objective, nominative, etc.), and, except for personal nouns (those that refer to people), they do not have specific plural forms. **Hon** *(book)*, for example, may refer to one or more books.

There are ways to show plurality if it is necessary to be specific. One way is by use of Counters *(See Chapter 39)* or words such as **takusan** *(a lot)* or **iroiro** *(various)*.

Another way is to repeat the noun, sometimes with a sound change in the repeated portion; for example, **shima** *(island)* is pluralized as **shima-jima**, **hito** *(person)* becomes **hito-bito**, **kuni** *(country)* becomes **kuni-guni**.

Personal nouns may be pluralized with the suffix **-tachi**, as in **seito-tachi** *(students)*. A person's name followed by **-tachi** refers to that person and his immediate group or family: **Suzuki-tachi** = "Suzuki et al."

PRONOUNS

Pronouns also do not change for case. **Watakushi**, for instance, can be translated "I" or "me."

Both personal pronouns and demonstrative pronouns have specific plural forms. *(See below and Chapter 20, Demonstrative Forms.)*

PERSONAL PRONOUNS

	Singular	Plural
1st person:	**watakushi** *(I, me)*	**watakushi-tachi** *(we, us)*
2nd person:	**anata** *(you)*	**anata-tachi** or **anata-gata** *(you, you-all)*
3rd person:	**kare** *(he, him)* **kanojo** *(she, her)* **ano hito** *(he, she, that person)*	**karera** *(they*—masc. or mixed*)* **kanojo-tachi** *(they*—fem.*)* **ano hitobito** or **ano hito-tachi** *(they, those people)*

Watakushi is often shortened to **watashi** or (for women) **atashi**. Men and boys often use the word **boku** (plural **bokura** or **boku-tachi**) instead of **watakushi**. **Boku** is more casual than **watakushi** or **watashi**.

Frequently the name, title, or position of the listener is used instead of **anata**.

Ex.: **Tanaka-san wa Nihon no kata desu ka?**
    Mr. Tanaka, are you from Japan? (Lit. Is Mr. Tanaka a Japanese person?)
    Sensei wa ima isogashii desu ka?
    Teacher, are you busy? (Lit. Is the teacher busy?)

There are various other words used for "you" and "I," depending on the formal or casual nature of the situation and on the relationship between the speaker and the listener. *(See below, Forms of Address.)*

Forms of Address

The honorific suffix -**san** is placed after the name (usually the surname) of the person being addressed. This suffix is often compared to "Mr.," "Mrs.," etc., but in reality it has no reference to gender or marital status. **San** should *never* be used after the speaker's own name.

-**Sama** is a more honorific form of the same suffix. *(See Chapter 36, Honorifics.)* -**Chan** is a diminutive form of -**san**, used after the name (usually the given name) of a close friend or younger family member. -**Kun** is a casual suffix used after the name of friends and peers in a casual situation.

A woman may address her husband (or intended husband) as **anata**, instead of his name. The man is more likely to call his wife or intended wife **omae** or **kimi**, both of which are also translated "you."

Family members may be addressed by position in the family. A person will address his older brother as **oniisan** *(older brother)* and his older sister as **onēsan** *(older sister)* more often than he will call them by their names. Younger siblings are also sometimes addressed as **imōto** *(younger sister)* or **otōto** *(younger brother)*, but more often they are called by their first names.

Even people who are not members of one's own family are often called by family relationship words: a young woman in her teens or early twenties may be called **onēsan**, particularly if the speaker is a stranger and does not know her name. A young man may be called **oniisan**; a woman who looks like she might be someone's wife or mother may be called **okusan** *(wife)* or **okāsan** *(mother)* or, if she is a little older, **obasan** *(aunt)* or **obāsan** *(grandmother)*; a man may be called **ojisan** *(uncle)* or **ojiisan** *(grandfather)*.

Ellipsis (Omission of Words) & Clarification

It is common in normal Japanese conversation to omit personal pronouns and any item of information that has already been introduced or that may be understood from context. Personal pronouns that mean "I" and "you" are especially susceptible to this ellipsis. It is left up to the listener to assume from context who or what is referred to. If he does not understand, he may ask for a clarification, and this happens frequently in conversation.

Ex.: **A: Kesa nanji ni tsukimashita ka?**
      B: Watashi desu ka?
      A: Hai.
      A: What time did [you] arrive this morning?
      B: Me?
      A: Yes.

Although the English translation requires a pronoun to be spoken in the first sentence, the Japanese will normally omit it unless there is some over-riding reason to include it.

Also frequently, the Japanese will anticipate a possible need for clarification and add it at the end of a sentence, as an afterthought. This happens more often in casual conversation than in more formal speech.

Ex.: **Itta koto [ga] arimasu ka? —Hawai ni.**
      Have you ever been there? —to Hawaii.

This kind of afterthought/clarification is also used to add emphasis or to vent emotion.

Ex.: **Hazukashii no yo—watashi!**
      [I] am too embarrassed—I [am]!

Sentence Softening

To the Japanese it is considered abrupt or impolite to speak too clearly or in very definite terms. To avoid this they use various tactics to soften the tone of their speech. One tactic is to leave a sentence incomplete by ending it with **ga** or **keredomo** *(but/however)*. Another way is to add **no desu** or **n' desu** *(It is that . . .)* at the end of a sentence.

Yet another common tactic is to add **to omoimasu** *(I think)* at the end of the sentence. This does not necessarily mean that there is any doubt at all in the speaker's mind as to the truth of what he has said.

Ex.: **A: Suzuki-san wa imasen ka?**
      B: Mō kaerimashitan' desu ga, . . .
      A: Aa sō? Dō shita no desu ka?
      B: Chotto byōki datta to omoimasu ga, . . .
      A: Is Suzuki not in?
      B: He already went home, [but] . . .
      A: Really? Why is that?
      B: I think he was a little ill, [but] . . .

20. Demonstrative Forms

("KO-SO-A-DO")

The following pronoun, adjective, and adverb forms all follow a first-syllable pattern that indicates either position in relation to the speaker (**ko-** = close, **so-** = not so close, **a-** = at a greater distance) or a question (**do-**).

kore	sore	are	dore
this one	*that one*	*that one there*	*which one?*
korera	sorera	arera	dorera[1]
these [ones]	*those [ones]*	*those over there*	*which ones?*
kono [+ noun]	sono [+ noun]	ano [+ noun]	dono [+ noun]
this . . .	*that . . .*	*that . . . there*	*which . . .?*
koko	soko	asoko[2]	doko
here; this place	*there; that place*	*over there; that place there*	*where? what place?*
kochira	sochira	achira	dochira
this way; this direction	*that way; that direction*	*that way; that direction*	*which way? which direction?*
kō iu [+ noun]	sō iu [+ noun]	aa iu [+ noun]	dō iu [+ noun]
kono yō na . . .	sono yō na . . .	ano yō na . . .	dono yō na . . .
konna . . .	sonna . . .	anna . . .	donna . . .
this kind of . . .	*that kind of . . .*	*that kind of . . .*	*what kind of . . . ?*
konna ni	sonna ni	anna ni	donna ni
this [much]; to this degree	*that [much]; to that degree*	*that [much]; to that degree*	*how [much]? to what degree?*
kono yō ni	sono yō ni	ano yō ni	dono yō ni
kō	sō	aa	dō
like this; in this way	*like that; in that way*	*like that; in that way*	*how? in what way?*

[1] **Dorera** is rarely used; **dore** or **dochira** may be used instead.

[2] Another common word for **asoko** is **mukō**.

Ex.: **Kore wa hon desu.** *This is a book.*

Sorera wa anata no desu ka? *Are those yours?*

Dō iu kuruma ga suki desu ka? *What kind of cars do you like?*

Sonna kamera wa takai deshō.
That kind of camera is probably expensive.

Okāsan ga anna ni byōki da to omowanakatta desu.
I didn't think/realize that your mother was that sick.

Kono yō ni shite mo ii desu ka?
Is it okay to do it this way?

21. Particles

A particle (also called "post-position," "relational," or "grammar marker") tells the relationship of a word or phrase to the rest of the sentence. Sometimes this is similar to the function of a preposition in English ("of," "by," "to," "for," etc.), but not always.

A particle *always follows* the word or phrase it refers to but is not strictly part of that word. A particle has no meaning of its own outside its function as a relationship marker. In certain cases, two particles may be combined.

PARTICLES AND THEIR FUNCTIONS

de   Follows the agent or means of doing something

      Ex.:   **Itsumo pen de kakimasu.** *I always write with a pen.*
             Hikōki de itte kimashita. *I went and came back by plane.*
             Nihongo de hanashite kudasai. *Please speak in Japanese.*

Follows a counter or other word that tells "by" or "for" what amount, quantity, or number something is done.

      Ex.:   **Gohyaku-en de kaimashita.** *I bought it for 500 yen.*
             Sannin de ikimasu. *The three [of us] will go. ("by threes")*
             Kono shigoto wa jikan de haraimasu. *This job pays by the hour.*

Location indicator for action. Follows the location "in" or "at" which an action takes place or the area within which a statement is true.

      Ex.:   **Eki de matte imashita.** *I was waiting at the station.*
             Ginkō no mae de aimashō. *Let's meet in front of the bank.*
             Nihon de mottomo ōkii desu. *It is the biggest in Japan.*

Indicates when an activity or time period ends, how long an activity takes, or the age at which something happens to someone.

      Ex.:   **Kurasu wa kuji de owarimasu.** *The class ends at 9:00.*
             Kyō de rokkagetsu ni narimasu.
                It is (becomes) six months as of today.
             Gofun de dekiru to omoimasu.
                I think I can do it in five minutes.
             Sanjussai de kekkon shimashita.
                He got married at age 30.

Indicates a reason or purpose.

      Ex.:   **Shiken de isogashii desu.** *He's busy with exams.*
             Shigoto de Ōsaka ni itte kimashita. *He went to Osaka on business.*

Note: **De** should not be confused with the TE-form of **desu**. *(See Chapter 5.)*

e   Direction indicator: *to/towards, in/into, on/onto.* Follows the destination of motion. In this sense it is interchangeable with **ni.** (For other uses of **ni,** this particle is not used.)

Ex.:   **Otōsan wa senshū Hawai e ikimashita.**
Father went to Hawaii last week.
Nishi e mukatte kudasai. *Please face [towards] the west.*
O-namae o kono kami e kaite kudasai.
Please write your name on this paper.
Kyōshitsu e hairimashita. *He entered [into] the classroom.*

ga   Subject indicator. When the topic of the sentence is different from the grammatical subject, the grammatical subject is followed by **ga.** (The topic is followed by **wa.**)

Ex.:   **Ano heya ni wa jūroku-nin no hito ga imasu.**
In that room there are 16 people. (The location is the topic.)
O-tomodachi wa eigo ga jōzu desu.
Your friend is good at English. (Lit. As for your friend, [his] English is good.)

Certain verbs will dictate the use of **ga** as subject indicator.

Ex.:   **furu** *(fall, as rain or snow)*
Ame ga futte imasu. *It is raining.*

owaru *(end, be over)*
Kaigi ga owarimashita. *The meeting is over.*

suku *(be empty)*
Onaka ga sukimashita. *My stomach is empty. (I'm hungry.)*

Certain verbs and adjectives call for a grammatical subject where the corresponding English sentence would use a direct object. In these cases **ga** is used rather than the direct object particle **o.**

Ex.:   **aru** *(exist, be located)*
Watakushi wa pen ga arimasu.
I have a pen. (Lit. As for me, a pen exists.)

dekiru *(be able to do, be possible)*
Watakushi wa Nihongo ga dekimasu.
I can do Japanese. (Lit. As for me, Japanese is possible.)

hitsuyō [desu] *(be needed)*
Kuruma ga hitsuyō desu.
I need a car. (Lit. As for me, a car is needed.)

hoshii [desu] *(be wanted)*
Otōto wa hanbāgā ga hoshii desu.
Younger brother wants a hamburger. (Lit. As for younger brother, a hamburger is wanted.)

(ga)   **kikoeru** *(be audible)*
Ayashii oto ga kikoemashita.
I heard a suspicious sound. (Lit. . . . sound was audible.)

kirai [desu] *(be disliked/hated)*
Watakushi wa kōhii ga kirai desu.
I dislike coffee. (Lit. As for me, coffee is disliked.)

mieru *(be visible)*
Oka no ue kara, fune ga miemasu.
You can see the ship from the top of the hill. (Lit. The ship is visible . . .)

suki [desu] *(be liked)*
Watakushi wa chokorēto ga suki desu.
I like chocolate. (Lit. As for me, chocolate is liked.)

wakaru *(understand/be understood)*
Watakushi wa Nihongo ga wakarimasu.
I understand Japanese. (Lit. As for me, Japanese is understood.)

Ga replaces **wa** to put emphasis on the topic or to indicate a contrast.

Ex.:   **Kare ga Ōsaka ni ikimashita.**
He [is the one who] went to Osaka. (not someone else)

Exception: When **ga** would ordinarily be used but emphasis is called for or contrast is indicated, **ga** is replaced by **wa**.

Ex.:   **Enpitsu ga arimasu keredomo, keshigomu wa arimasen.**
I have a pencil, but I don't have an eraser. (Eraser receives emphasis by contrast.)

Ga replaces **wa** after a question word or phrase (**nani, dare, dono [hon]**, etc.). The response to such a question also is followed by **ga** instead of **wa**, since this in essence puts some emphasis on the answer.

Ex.:   **A: Dochira no tatemono ga toshokan desu ka?**
       B: Ano tatemono ga toshokan desu.
       A: Which building is the library?
       B: That building is the library.

Ga replaces **wa** when a topic is being introduced for the first time, as in a story or narrative of an experience.

Ex.:   **Aru hi, sei no takai otoko no hito ga kyōshitsu ni haitte kimashita.**
One day a tall man came into the classroom.

Subject indicator for subordinate clause. In a compound sentence, if the subject of a subordinate (dependent) clause is different from the subject of the main clause, the subject of the subordinate clause is followed by **ga.**

(ga) Ex.: **Okyaku-sama ga sugu kimasu node, okāsan wa totemo isogashii desu.** *Since guests are coming soon, Mother is very busy.*
Tenki ga yokereba, [watakushi-tachi wa] ashita shuppatsu shimasu. *If the weather is good, we will depart tomorrow.*

Note: If the subjects are the same, **wa** is used for both clauses, although one or the other subject is ordinarily omitted.

Ex.: **Suzuki-san wa byōki desu node, hayaku kaerimashita.**
Suzuki went home early, because he is sick.

Subject indicator for indirect quote.

Ex.: **[Kare wa] tomodachi ga konai to iimashita.**
He said his friend is not coming. (**Ga** indicates that **tomodachi** is the subject of **konai**; the subject of the main verb **iimashita** is assumed if it is not stated.)

Subject indicator for relative clause. Since a relative clause is always a dependent clause, **ga** is used to mark the subject, although it is sometimes replaced by **no.**

Ex.: **Suzuki-san ga kaita tegami wa asoko desu.**
Suzuki-san no kaita tegami wa asoko desu.
The letter that Suzuki wrote is over there.

ka   Question marker. After a verb, **ka** makes the sentence into a question.

Ex.: **Kore wa pen desu.** *This is a pen.*
Kore wa pen desu ka? *Is this a pen?*

In very casual conversation **ka** may follow a noun or a phrase in an incomplete sentence, to ask confirmation of information.

Ex.: **A: Are ga suki da yo.**
B: Nani ga–nattō ka? Sō ka?
 A: I really like that stuff.
 B: What–fermented beans? Really?

Ka is often used to express an "either/or" choice in a question or a statement.

Ex.: **Tanaka-san wa sensei desu ka? Gakusei desu ka?**
Is Tanaka a teacher or [is he] a student?

Ka may follow a choice of nouns, in which case the **ka** after the final noun may be omitted.

Ex.: **Chokorēto ka banira ka, dochira ga hoshii desu ka?**
Which do you want–chocolate or vanilla?
Densha ka takushii [ka] de ikimasu.
I will go either by train or by taxi.

(ka) If **ka** follows a choice of verbs within a sentence, the verbs should be in the Informal Form.

> Ex.: **Iku ka ikanai ka, kimenai to ikemasen.**
> *You have to decide whether to go or not to go.*

In some cases only one of the choices may be expressed, as when asking if/whether something is true.

> Ex.: **Imōto wa dekakete mo ii ka to kikimashita.**
> *Younger sister asked if it's okay to go out.*

kara   Direction indicator: *from.* Follows an origin, source, or beginning point.

> Ex.: **Ōsaka kara kimashita.** *He came from Osaka.*
> **Tomodachi kara tegami o moraimashita.**
> *I got a letter from a friend.*
> **Ichiji kara niji-han made benkyō shimasu.**
> *I will study from 1:00 to 2:30.*

Kara is often paired with **made** *(up to).*

> Ex.: **Koko kara asoko no ki made hashirimashō.**
> *Let's run from here to the tree over there.*

(See Chapter 22, Conjunctions, for KARA as a conjunction.)

made   *until, up to, as far as, through.* Refers to time or space.

> Ex.: **San-peiji made yomimashita.**
> *I read through page three.*
> **Yūbinkyoku made aruite kimasu.**
> *I will walk as far as the post office [and come back].*
> **Mainichi jūichiji made benkyō shimasu.**
> *I study until 11:00 every day.*

Often paired with **kara** *(from).*

> Ex.: **Yoru jūji kara asa kuji-han made nemashita.**
> *He slept from 10:00 at night to 9:30 in the morning.*

May follow a verb (V3) to mean "until [I] do."

> Ex.: **Otōsan ga kaeru made machimashō.**
> *Let's wait until Father returns.*

Following a counter, this particle is translated "as many as," "as much as," or "up to."

> Ex.: **Kono basu wa nijūgo-nin made noreru sō desu.**
> *I understand that this bus will hold as many as 25 people.*
> *(Lit. As many as 25 people can board . . .)*

made ni   *by [a certain time]*

> Ex.: **Sanji made ni denwa o shite kudasai.** *Please telephone by 3:00.*
> **Getsuyōbi made ni owaru no wa muri da to omoimasu.**
> *I think it's impossible to finish by Monday.*

After a verb (V3), this means "by the time that [I] do."

> Ex.: **Kurasu ga hajimaru made ni kore o anki shinakereba narimasen.**
> *I have to memorize this by the time class starts.*

mo   Adjunct marker. In a list of two or more items, **mo** adds emphasis to each item and can be translated "both" or "as well [as]." With a negative verb, it means "either/or" or "neither/nor." **Mo** in this usage supersedes other particles.

> Ex.: **Oniisan mo onēsan mo kuru to omoimasu.**
> *I think both older brother and older sister are coming.*
> **Pen mo enpitsu mo chōku mo kono hako ni irete arimasu.**
> *Both pens and pencils, as well as chalk, are kept in this box.*
> **Kuruma mo jitensha mo arimasen.**
> *I don't have either a car or a bicycle.*

When **mo** follows a single item, it means "also," "too," or "as well."

> Ex.: **Oniisan mo kuru to omoimasu.**
> *I think older brother is coming, too.*
> **Bōrupen mo arimasu.** *There are ball-point pens, also.*

Mo may follow certain other particles without altering the function of the other particle or itself.

> Ex.: **Tōkyō ni mo ikimashita.** *I went to Tokyo, also.*
> **Kōba de mo hatarakimasu.** *He works in the factory, as well.*
> **Amerika kara mo hito ga kuru hazu desu.**
> *People are supposed to be coming from America, too.*

After a counter, **mo** may indicate "as many as" or "[not] even."

> Ex.: **Ano hito wa kanji o sanzen mo shitte imasu ga, watakushi wa hitotsu mo yomemasen.**
> *He knows as many as 3,000 kanji, but I can't read even one.*

(See also Chapter 24, Interrogatives + KA, MO, DEMO.)

na   Quasi Adjective marker. *(See also Chapter 25, Adjectives.)*

> Ex.: **O-tomodachi wa totemo kirei na hito desu, ne.**
> *Your friend is a very pretty person, isn't she?*

nado   *and so on, et cetera, for example, and things like that*

> Ex.: **Supōtsu wa, sakkā nado ga suki desu.**
> *As for sports, I like soccer, for example.*

(nado)   Kōkōsei no toki, sūgaku ya kokugo nado o benkyō shimashita.
When I was a high school student, I studied math, language, and things like that.

Sometimes follows a series marked by **toka**.

Ex.: Supōtsu wa, yakyū toka, ragubii toka, sakkā nado ga suki desu.
As for sports, I like things like baseball, rugby, and soccer, for example.

ni   Direction indicator: *to/towards* a destination or direction or *into* an area or structure. In this use **ni** and **e** are interchangeable.

Ex.: Ashita Tōkyō ni ikimasu. *Tomorrow I will go to Tokyo.*
Migi ni magatte kudasai. *Please turn to[wards] the right.*
Chōdo yoji ni yūbinkyoku ni hairimashita.
I entered the post office at exactly 4:00.

Indirect object indicator: *to/for [someone or some thing]*

Ex.: O-tomodachi ni denwa o shite kudasai. *Please phone your friend.*
Okāsan ni tegami o kakimashita.
I wrote my mother a letter. (I wrote a letter to my mother.)

Specific time indicator: *at/on/in [a time]*

Ex.: Gogatsu tsuitachi ni shuppatsu shimasu. *We will depart on May 1.*
Hachiji-han ni denwa o suru to iimashita.
He said he will phone at 8:30.
Sen-kyūhyaku-rokujūni-nen ni umaremashita.
I was born in 1962.
Fuyu ni yoku sukii o shimasu. *I go skiing a lot in the winter.*

Location indicator: existence *in/at* a place when an existence verb is used. *(See Chapter 33, Relative Positions, for existence verbs.)*

Ex.: Otōsan wa ima ni imasu. *Father is in the living room.*
Shinbun wa asoko ni arimasu. *The newspaper is over there.*
Tanaka-san wa Tōkyō ni sunde imasu. *Tanaka lives in Tokyo.*
Koko ni tatte mo ii desu ka? *Is it okay to stand here?*

On/onto [a surface]

Ex.: O-namae o akasen no ue ni kaite kudasai.
Please write your name on [top of] the red line.
Sensei wa bunshō o kokuban ni kakimashita.
The teacher wrote a sentence on the blackboard.

Agency indicator with Passive verbs: *by/from*

Ex.: Saifu wa dorobō ni nusumaremashita.
The wallet was stolen by a thief.

(ni) Object indicator with a Causative verb. Comes after the person who is being caused or allowed to do something. *(See also Particle O.)*

Ex.: **Watakushi ni makasete kudasai.** *Please leave it to me.*
Tanaka-san wa musuko ni (or **o**) **mise ni ikasemashita.**
Tanaka made his son go to the store.

Source indicator with **morau** or **Vte + morau**.

Ex.: **Tomodachi ni hana o moraimashita.**
I received some flowers from a friend.
Mori-sensei ni oshiete moraimasu.
I will have Professor Mori teach me.

Used after a Quasi or Noun + NO Adjective to create an adverb. *(See Chapter 27, Adverbs.)*

no   Possessive indicator. **No** follows the possessor and precedes the item in possession; it takes the same position as 'S in English.

Ex.: **Kore wa Tanaka-san no saifu desu.** *This is Tanaka's wallet.*
Kare no denwa bangō o oshiete kudasai.
Please tell me his phone number.
Watakushi no desu. *It is mine.*

No also can make a noun or noun phrase into an adjective/adj. phrase.

Ex.: **Sore wa Nihon no kaisha desu, ne.**
That is a Japanese company, isn't it?
Sūgaku no kyōkasho o kaimashita ka?
Did you buy a math textbook?

Note: The particle **no** should not be confused with the **no** that makes a verb into a noun. *(See Chapter 18, Informal Endings: NO.)*

o   Direct object indicator. Follows the noun or noun phrase that receives the direct action of the verb.

Ex.: **Kippu o kaimashita.** *I bought a ticket.*
Chūka-ryōri o tabetai desu. *I want to eat Chinese food.*

In verb phrases where a direct object is included with the verb **suru** (**denwa o suru, kaimono o suru, ryokō o suru,** etc.), the **o** is often eliminated, resulting in a two-word verb (**denwa suru, kaimono suru, ryokō suru**).

In/along/through/over/across [a street, bridge, space, etc.]

Ex.: **Yoru osoku made michi o arukimashita.**
He walked [along] the streets until late at night.
Hashi o watatte migi ni magarimasu.
You cross [over] the bridge and turn right.
Tori wa ike no ue o tobimashita. *The birds flew over the pond.*

(o)   Indicates the point *at* which a turn is made.

Ex.: **Soko no kado o hidari ni magatte kudasai.**
Turn left at the corner there.
Depāto o kita e magarimasu.
[You] turn north at the department store.

Indicates the place *from/out of* which someone departs.

Ex.: **Mainichi kuji ni uchi o demasu.**
He leaves the house at 9:00 every day.
Basu o orite, arukimashita. *I got off the bus and walked.*
Ōsaka o hanareta toki sabishikatta desu.
When I left Osaka, I was sad.

Indicates the cause for some human emotion.

Ex.: **Nagai aida okāsan ga shinda koto o kanashimimashita.**
He mourned his mother's death for a long time.
Raishū nyūin suru no o shinpai shite imasu.
I am worried (worrying) about going into the hospital next week.

to   Adjunct marker. Follows each item except the last in a list that is considered to be complete.

Ex.: **Ano heya ni wa Nihonjin to Amerikajin ga imasu.**
In that room there are Japanese and Americans (no others).
Tanaka-san to Suzuki-san wa ano heya ni imasu.
Tanaka and Suzuki are in that room. (The speaker is concerned with only Tanaka and Suzuki, so the list is considered complete.)

The last item in the list may be followed by **to** plus whatever other particle is appropriate. This adds some emphasis to the items in the list, but not as much as when using **mo**.

Ex.: **Pen to enpitsu to chōku to wa kono hako ni irete arimasu.**
The pens, the pencils, and the chalk are kept in this box.

When **to** follows a single item, it takes the meaning "together with" or "along with."

Ex.: **Oniisan to kimashita.** *He came with his older brother.*
Seito to hanashite kudasai. *Please speak with the student.*

[The same] as, [different] from, [similar] to

Ex.: **Kono pen wa are to onaji desu.** *This pen is the same as that one.*
Ano kamera wa kore to chotto chigaimasu.
That camera differs a little from this one.
Yukiko wa hontō ni okāsan to nite imasu.
Yukiko really looks like (is similar to) her mother.

(to)   Quotation marker. Follows a direct or indirect quotation.

>   Ex.:   **Ashita kuru to iimashita.** *He said that he will come tomorrow.*
>   **"Ashita kimasu" to iimashita.** *He said, "I will come tomorrow."*

Follows a word that describes a sound.

>   Ex.:   **Yukiko wa batan to mado o shimete, heya o demashita.**
>   *Yukiko closed the window with a bang and left the room.*

Used instead of **ni** in certain adverb expressions.

>   Ex.:   **Gaijin ni yukkuri to hanashite kudasai.**
>   *Please speak slowly to foreigners.*
>   **Minna wa ukiuki to hanashiatte imashita.**
>   *Everyone was talking cheerfully with one another.*
>   **Basu wa pittari to tomarimashita.** *The bus came to a dead stop.*

toka   *things like, for example, and so on. (See also NADO.)*

>   Ex.:   **Mainichi yomu no wa, shinbun toka, zasshi toka, manga toka
>   o yomimasu.**
>   *As for things that I read every day, I read newspapers,
>   magazines, and comics, for example.*
>   **Yoru wa, ongaku o kiku toka, hon o yomu toka shimasu.**
>   *In the evenings I do things like listening to music, reading
>   books, and so on.*

tte   Idiomatic Casual marker for reported speech.

>   Ex.:   **Zenzen dekinai tte.** *(Casual) He says he can't do it at all.*

wa   Topic indicator. Follows the person or thing under discussion in the
sentence. "As for" may be used in translation. There may be more
than one topic in a sentence.

>   Ex.:   **Kore wa pen desu.** *This is a pen.*
>   **Watakushi wa Nihongo ga wakarimasu.**
>   *I understand Japanese. (Lit. As for me, Japanese is understood.)*
>   **Haru wa, hana ga sakimasu.**
>   *In spring the flowers bloom. (Lit. As for spring, flowers
>   bloom.)*

When **wa** follows another particle, it indicates that the topic includes
that particle.

>   Ex.:   **Ano heya de wa, shachō-san wa okyaku-sama to hanashite imasu.**
>   *In that room the company president is talking with a visitor.*
>   (The topic is "in that room.")

Replaces other particles when a contrast or mild emphasis is called for.

>   Ex.:   **Nōto o kaimashita ga, pen wa kaimasen deshita.**
>   *I bought a notebook, but I didn't buy any pens.*

(wa)   **Pen ga arimasen keredomo, enpitsu wa arimasu.**
              I don't have a pen, but I do have a pencil.

May replace other particles when there is no need to be specific about
the function of a word.

Ex.:   **Ranchi wa, mō tabemashita ka?**
       Did you already eat lunch? (Lit. As for lunch, did you . . . ?)
       O-tomodachi wa yūbe aimashita.
       I met your friend last night. (Lit. As for your friend, I met . . .)

Sometimes used instead of the emphatic **yo** in casual feminine speech.

Ex.:   **Dame da wa!** *(Casual)*
       Don't do that! (Lit. It's bad!)

Note: **Wa** is *never* used after a question word or phrase (**nani, dare, dono**
[hon], etc.), but is always replaced by **ga**.

ya   Adjunct marker. Follows each item except the last in a possibly
          incomplete list. **Ya** is never used after the final item in the list.

Ex.:   **Ano heya ni wa Amerika-jin ya Kanada-jin ga imasu.**
       In that room there are Americans and Canadians (and possibly
       others).
       Bōrupen ya mannenhitsu wa kono hako ni irete arimasu.
       Ball-point pens and fountain pens (and things like that) are
       kept in this box.

yo   Emphasis marker. Placed after the final verb to add emphasis to a
          sentence, similar to an exclamation point. Sometimes is translated
          "you know," to verbalize the emphasis.

Ex.:   **Okane ga nai desu yo.**
       I don't have any money! (I don't have any money, you know.)

yori   from [a point in time or space]

Ex.:   **Akasen yori ue ni wa kakanaide kudasai.**
       Please don't write above the red line. (Lit. . . . from the red
       line upwards.)
       Nijihan yori mae ni kite wa ikemasen.
       You mustn't come before 2:30.

Comparison: *[more] than.* Often followed by **mo** and/or paired with
[no] hō ga. *(See also Chapter 28, Comparisons.)*

Ex.:   **Kono hon wa are yori omoshiroi desu.**
       This book is more interesting than that one.
       Ninjin yori oishii desu.
       It's better [tasting] than carrots.
       Chokorēto yori mo banira no hō ga suki desu.
       I like vanilla more than chocolate.

22. Conjunctions

A conjunction makes a connection between words, phrases, or clauses. Some conjunctions change the direction of the sentence or introduce a new or contrasting thought.

dakara   *therefore, because of that, that's why.* Begins a new sentence. (from **desu kara**)

Ex.: **Asagohan o tabemasen deshita. Dakara onaka ga suite imasu.**
I didn't eat breakfast. That's why I'm hungry.

demo   *however; yes, but* . . . Introduces a new sentence.

Ex.: **Kesa denwa o shimashita. Demo rusu deshita kara, ato de mata denwa o shite mimasu.**
I phoned this morning. But there was no answer, so I will try phoning again later.

ga   *but, however.* Essentially interchangeable with **keredomo**. Comes at the end of a main clause.

Ex.: **O-mise ni ikimashita ga, nanimo kaimasen deshita.**
I went to the store, but I didn't buy anything.

Sometimes **ga** is placed after the final verb to indicate an incomplete thought or to soften a sentence.

Ex.: **Shitsurei desu ga,** . . . *Excuse me, but* . . .
Suzuki-san wa kyō o-yasumi desu ga, . . .
Mr. Suzuki is off [work] today, but . . .

kara   *because, since.* Follows the subordinate clause that indicates the cause or reason for something. In this sense **kara** is interchangeable with **node**. *(See Chapter 21, Particles for KARA as "from/since.")*

Ex.: **Byōki desu kara, hayaku kaerimashita.**
He went home early, because he is sick.

keredomo   *but, however.* Comes at the end of a main clause. Essentially interchangeable with **ga**. Alternative forms: **kedo, kedomo, keredo.**

Ex.: **O-mise ni ikimashita keredomo, nanimo kaimasen deshita.**
I went to the store, but I didn't buy anything.

mata   *also.* Essentially interchangeable with **soshite**. Introduces a new thought or sentence. *(See Chapter 27, Adverbs, for MATA as "again.")*

Ex. **Hawai ni tomarimashita. Mata, Arasuka ni mo ikimashita.**
He stopped over in Hawaii. And he also went to Alaska.

moshi   *if.* Begins a sentence and requires a verb in some conditional form.

> Ex.:   **Moshi sensei ga konai to shitara, dō shimashō ka?**
> *If it happened that the teacher didn't come, what should we do?*

nazenara[ba]   *because.* Begins an explanation of the previous statement. *(Lit. "If [you ask] why, . . .)*

> Ex.:   **Yukiko wa kyō chotto sabishii desu. Nazenara, bōifurendo ga kinō hikkoshite shimaimashita.**
> *Yukiko is a little sad today. It's because her boyfriend moved away yesterday.*

node   *because, since.* Comes at the end of a subordinate clause that indicates the cause or reason for something. Essentially interchangeable with **kara** in this sense.

> Ex.:   **Yōji ga mada arimasu node, hachiji goro made kaerimasen.**
> *Since I still have things to do, I won't go home until about 8:00.*

shi   *and what's more, not only . . . but also, so.* Comes after the verb (usually in an Informal form) of any clause except the final one.

> Ex.:   **O-tenki ga ii shi, tomodachi mo iru shi, totemo ureshii desu.**
> *The weather is fine, and my friends are with me, so I am really happy.*

shikashi   *however.* Begins a new and contrasting thought.

> Ex.:   **Hawai ni tomarimashita. Shikashi o-tomodachi ni denwa o shimasen deshita.**
> *I stopped over in Hawaii. However, I didn't phone your friend.*

soredemo   *despite that.* Begins a sentence, but refers to the previous statement.

> Ex.:   **A: Suzuki-san wa saikin byōki da sō desu.**
> **B: Sō ne. Soredemo mainichi kaisha ni kite imasu.**
> *A: I hear that Suzuki's been sick lately.*
> *B: That's right. Despite that, he is coming to the company every day.*

sorede[wa]   *therefore, because of that.* Begins a sentence, but refers to the previous statement.

> Ex.:   **A: Kaisha wa totemo isogashii desu yo.**
> **B: Sorede denwa o shinai no desu ka?**
> *A: It's awfully busy [at] the company.*
> *B: Is that why you haven't phoned? (Lit. . . . don't phone?)*

sorekara   *after that, then.* Begins a sentence, but refers to the previous statement.

Ex.:   **Eki o dete, migi ni magarimasu. Sorekara shingō made aruite, soko de matte kudasai.**

You leave the station and turn right. Then walk up to the traffic signal and wait there.

sorenara   *if that is the case, if that's so.* Begins a sentence, but refers to the previous statement.

Ex.:   **Ame ga furisō desu. Sorenara kasa o motte dekaketa hō ga ii to omoimasu.**

It looks like it's going to rain. If that's the case, I think it's best to take an umbrella.

soretomo   *or, or else, otherwise.* Begins a sentence that indicates an alternative to something in the previous sentence.

Ex.:   **Konban dekakeru no desu ka? Soretomo hayaku nemasu ka?**

Are you going out this evening? Or will you go to bed early?

sō shitara   *if that is so, if [you] do that, that being the case.* Begins a sentence, but refers to the previous statement.

Ex.:   A: **Ashita Ōsaka ni iku yotei desu.**
B: **Sō shitara, chotto o-negai dekimasu ka?**

A: I'm planning to go to Osaka tomorrow.
B: If that's so, can I ask you to do something for me?

soshite   *also, and also.* Introduces a new sentence or thought and makes a mild reference to the previous statement.

Ex.:   **Asa hayaku okite, benkyō shimashita. Soshite gakkō made arukimashita.**

I got up early in the morning and studied. And also I walked up to the school.

suru to   *then, thereupon, at that point, that being done.* The sentence that follows this phrase is a statement of something that might naturally follow the action described in the previous sentence. It will not be a request, command, or suggestion.

Ex.:   A: **Shachō-san wa kyō imasen.**
B: **Suru to, niji no kaigi ni shusseki shinai no desu, ne.**

A: The company president isn't in today.
B: Then he will not attend the 2:00 meeting, will he?

23. Interrogatives

Japanese interrogatives are used to ask questions, *not* to construct relative clauses as in English. *(See Chapter 31, Relative Clauses.)* Many of the following interrogatives were presented with other Demonstrative Forms in Chapter 20.

dare   *who?*

> Ex.: **Dare ga unten shimashita ka?** *Who drove?*
> **Ano hito wa dare desu ka?** *Who is that person?*
> **Dare to ikimasu ka?** *With whom are you going?*

dochira   *which one? which way/direction?*

> Ex.: **Dochira ga hoshii desu ka?** *Which one do you want?*
> **Yūbinkyoku wa dochira e ikeba ii desu ka?**
> *Which way do I go to get to the post office? (Lit. As for the post office, which way is it good if I go?)*

dō iu   *what kind of . . . ?*

> Ex.: **Dō iu kamera o motte imasu ka?**
> *What kind of camera do you own?*
> **Tanaka-san wa dō iu hito desu ka?**
> *What kind of person is Tanaka?*

doko   *where?*

> Ex.: **Doko e ikimasu ka?** *Where are you going?*
> **Toshokan wa doko desu ka?** *Where is the library?*
> **Doko no hito desu ka?**
> *Where is he from? (Lit. He is a person of/from where?)*

donata   *who?* More formal than **dare**.

> Ex.: **Donata ga sutēki o chūmon nasaimashita ka?** *(Exalted)*
> *Who ordered the steak?*
> **Mō hitori no kata wa donata deshō ka?** *(Exalted)*
> *Who is the other person [in your party]?*

donna   *what kind of . . . ?*

> Ex.: **Donna kuruma ga suki desu ka?** *What kind of cars do you like?*
> **Donna hito ga koko ni sumu no desu ka?**
> *What kind of people will be living here?*

dono   *which . . . ?*

> Ex.: **Dono hon ga kanojo no desu ka?** *Which book is hers?*
> **Dono hito ga hanashimashita ka?** *Which person spoke?*

dono gurai/dono kurai   *about how much/many?*

> Ex.:   **Jikan wa dono gurai kakarimasu ka?**
> > *About how much time will it take?*
> **Okane wa dono gurai motte imasu ka?**
> > *About how much money do you have?*

dono yō na   *what kind of . . . ?*

> Ex.:   **Sensei wa dono yō na hito desu ka?**
> > *What kind of person is the teacher?*
> **Dono yō na mono o utte imasu ka?**
> > *What kind of things are they selling?*

dono yō ni   *in what way? how?*

> Ex.:   **O-nigiri no tsukurikata wa, dono yō ni shimasu ka?**
> > *How do you make o-nigiri? (Lit. As for the way you make o-nigiri, how do you do it?)*

dore   *which one?*

> Ex.:   **Dore ga pen desu ka?**
> > *Which one is the pen? (out of a choice of two or more)*

dōshite   *why?*

> Ex.:   **Okāsan wa dōshite konai no desu ka?**
> > *Why is it that your mother isn't coming?*
> **Dōshite chokorēto o tabemasen ka?**
> > *Why do you not eat chocolate?*

ikura   *how much?*

> Ex.:   **Sono ōkii hō wa ikura desu ka?**   *How much is that big one?*
> **Ikura no okane ga hitsuyō desu ka?**
> > *How much money do you need?*

ikutsu   *how many?*

> Ex.:   **Tokei wa ikutsu arimasu ka?**   *How many watches do you have?*

> Idiomatic: **[O-]ikutsu desu ka?**   *How old are [you]?*

itsu   *when?*

> Ex.:   **O-tanjōbi wa itsu desu ka?**   *When is your birthday?*
> **Itsu ga ii desu ka?**   *When is a good time?*

nan/nani   *what? (See also Chapter 39, Counters.)*

> Ex.:   **Sore wa nan desu ka?**   *What is that?*
> **Nani ga ichiban suki desu ka?**   *What do you like most?*
> **Are wa nan no hon desu ka?**   *What [kind of] book is that?*

naze   *why?* Essentially interchangeable with **dōshite**.

> Ex.:   **Kare wa naze kimasen deshita ka?**   *Why did he not come?*

24. Interrogative + <u>ka</u>, <u>mo</u>, <u>demo</u>

The chart below shows how **ka**, **mo**, and **demo** affect interrogatives in a fairly regular pattern.

Interrogative	Indefinite	Negative	Distributive
dare **donata** *who?*	**dare ka** **donata ka** *someone*	**dare mo** **donata mo** *no one, not anyone*	**dare demo** **donata demo** *anyone, no matter who*
dō[1] *how?*	**dō ka** *somehow*	**dō ni mo**[2] *in no way, not anyhow*	**dō demo** *anyhow, no matter how*
dochira *where? in what direction?*	**dochira ka** *somewhere, in some direction*	**dochira mo** *nowhere, in neither direction*	**dochira demo** *anywhere, in any direction*
doko *where?*	**doko ka** *somewhere*	**doko mo** *nowhere, not anywhere*	**doko demo** *anywhere, no matter where*
donna [+ Noun] *what kind of...?*	**donna [N] ka** *some kind of...*	**donna [N] mo** *no kind of... not any kind of...*	**donna [N] demo** *any kind of..., no matter what kind of...*
dono [+ Noun] *which...?*	**dono [N] ka** *some...*	**Dono [N] mo** *no..., not any...*	**Dono [N] demo** *any..., no matter which...*
dore *which one?*	**dore ka** *one of [them], one or other*	**dore mo** *none of [them], neither one*	**dore demo** *any of [them], whichever one*
ikura *how much?*	**ikura ka** *some [amount]*	**ikura mo** *almost none, hardly any*[3]	**ikura demo** *any amount, no matter how much*
ikutsu *how many?*	**ikutsu ka** *some [number]*	**ikutsu mo**[4] *none, not any*	**ikutsu demo** *any [number], however many*

(Chart continues on next page.)

(Chart continued from previous page.)

itsu *when?*	itsu ka *sometime*	kesshite[5] *never*	itsu demo *any time, whenever*
nan, nani *what?*	**nani ka** *something*	**nani mo** *nothing*	**nan demo** *anything*
nan [+ Counter][6] *how many...?*	**nan [C] ka** *so many..., some # of...*	**nan [C] mo** *no..., not any number of...*	**nan [C] demo** *however many..., any number of...*

[1] **Ikaga** is a more formal form of "how?" **Ikaga** is not used with **ka, mo, demo.**
[2] Note this exceptional form instead of **dō mo.**
[3] Note exceptional usage of **ikura mo.**
[4] With positive verb, **ikutsu mo** means "several."
[5] Exceptional: **itsumo** = *always*
Idiomatic: **itsumademo** = *forever*

Example sentences:

INDEFINITE

> **Dare ka ga denwa o shimashita.**   *Somebody telephoned.*
> **Doko ka e ikimashō ka?**   *Shall we go somewhere?*
> **Ikutsu ka kawasete itadakemasu ka?**   *May I buy some?*
> **Nani ka tabetai to omoimasu.**   *I think I would like to eat something.*
> **Kasa wa nanbon nokotte iru ka wakarimasen.**
> *I don't know how many umbrellas are left.*

NEGATIVE (**Daremo** and **nanimo** are used only with a negative verb or adjective; others may be used with either negative or positive.)

> **Dare mo kimasen deshita.**   *Nobody came.*
> **Dō ni mo dekinai to omoimasu.**   *I think there's no way it can be done.*
> **Doko ni mo ikimasen.**   *I'm not going anywhere.*
> **Nanimo hoshikunai desu.**   *I don't want anything.*
> **Okane wa ikura mo motte imasen.**   *I have hardly any money.*
> **Tokei o ikutsu mo motte imasu.**   *I have several watches.*

DISTRIBUTIVE

> **Dare demo kono hon ga suki da to omoimasu.**
> *I think anybody would like this book.*
> **Dono kamera demo takai desu.**   *Any camera would be expensive.*
> **Dore demo ii to omoimasu.**   *I think either one of them is okay.*
> **Ikura demo kamaimasen.**   *However much it is, it doesn't matter.*
> **Nan demo taberaremasu.**   *I can eat anything.*

25. Adjectives

There are three kinds of Japanese adjectives: **True** Adjectives, **Quasi** Adjectives, and **Noun + NO** Adjectives.

TRUE ADJECTIVES

True Adjectives **always end in the <u>syllable I</u>** in the Dictionary Form.

Examples:

atsui_ *(hot)*	samui_ *(cold)*
ōkii_ *(big)*	chiisai_ *(small)*
atarashii_ *(new)*	furui_ *(old)*
yasui_ *(cheap)*	takai_ *(expensive, high, tall)*

True Adjectives **are conjugated** as if they were verbs. The endings shown for the conjugated example below are the same for all True Adjectives.

Present positive	**atsui_** *(is hot)*
Past positive	**atsu<u>katta</u>** *(was hot)*
Present negative	**atsu<u>kunai</u>/atsu<u>kuarimasen</u>*** *(is not hot)*
Past negative	**atsu<u>kunakatta</u>/atsu<u>kuarimasen</u> deshita***
	(was not hot)

Exception: **Ii** *(good)* is never conjugated; its equal conjugatable counterpart is **yoi**.

Idiomatic: **Yokatta desu** *(It was good.)* is also used to express the feeling "Thank goodness" or "It turned out all right."

Even in its conjugated forms, a True Adjective **does not require a particle** when placed in front of a noun. Starred forms above (**-kuarimasen*** and **-kuarimasen deshita***) are not used before a noun or with Informal endings.

Ex.: **atarashii kutsu** *(new shoes)*
atarashikunai kutsu *(not-new shoes)*
omoshiroi koto *(something interesting)*
omoshirokunai koto *(something uninteresting)*

In casual conversation a sentence may end with a True Adjective; however, in the Normal-polite level of speech, the adjective should be followed by **desu**.

Ex.: **Takai, ne!** *It's expensive, isn't it! (Casual)*
Takai desu, ne! *It's expensive, isn't it! (Normal-polite)*

Kinō wa atsukatta. *Yesterday was hot. (Casual)*
Kinō wa atsukatta desu. *Yesterday was hot. (Normal-polite)*

QUASI ADJECTIVES
Quasi Adjectives may **end in any syllable, including I.**

Examples:

kirei *(pretty)*	**genki** *(healthy, lively)*
benri *(convenient)*	**fuben** *(inconvenient)*
suki *(liked, loved)*	**kirai** *(disliked, hated)*

A Quasi Adjective **cannot be conjugated.** Past tense, negative, etc., must be indicated by conjugating **desu.**

Ex.: **Ano hito wa kirei desu.** *That person is pretty.*
Ano hito wa kirei dewa arimasen. *That person is not pretty.*
Kirei dewanai hito wa heya ni hairimashita.
A not-pretty person entered the room.

A Quasi Adjective **must be followed by the particle na** when placed in front of a noun.

Ex.: **benri na apāto** *(convenient apartment)*
suki na hito *(the person [I] like; lit. "liked person")*

A True Adjective can be changed to a Quasi Adjective by dropping the final **i** of the present positive form and adding **na.** This is done only when the adjective is placed immediately before the noun it describes, and it is especially common with certain high-frequency adjectives, particularly **ōkii** and **chiisai**: **ōki na uchi** *(big house)*, **chiisa na kawa** *(small river)*.

NOUN + NO ADJECTIVES
Noun + NO Adjectives are **technically nouns** but are most often **used as adjectives** and are frequently compound words.

Ex.: **byōki** *(sick)*
toshiyori *(old, advanced in years)*
kanemochi *(rich)*

A Noun + NO Adjective **must be followed by NO** when placed before a noun.

Ex.: **byōki no hito** *(sick person)*
kanemochi no tomodachi *(rich friend)*

Like Quasi Adjectives, a Noun + NO Adjective **cannot be conjugated.** Past tense, negative, etc., must be indicated by conjugating **desu.**

Ex.: **Ano hito wa byōki desu.** *That person is sick.*
Ano hito wa byōki dewa arimasen. *That person is not sick.*
Byōki dewanai hito wa mō kaerimashita.
The not-sick person went home already.

26. Adjective Endings

Many of the same endings that are used with verbs can be used with adjectives, along with some endings that are not normally used with verbs.

An ending is usually attached to the stem of the True Adjective, although some endings follow the Informal Form, which is simply the adjective (in any conjugation) without **desu**. The stem is found by removing the final syllable (always **i**), as shown below:

True Adjective	Stem
atsui *(hot)*	**atsu-**
furui *(old)*	**furu-**
ōi *(plentiful)*	**ō-**
ōkii *(big)*	**ōki-**
yasashii *(easy)*	**yasashi-**

The stem of a True Adjective never changes.

Remember that True Adjectives include verb endings [V1 +] **nai**; [V2 +] **tai, nikui** and **yasui**; [Vte +] **hoshii**; [Vinf +] **mitai/rashii**. Quasi Adjectives include [V2 +] **sō** and [Vinf +] **yō**.

Following is a selection of common adjective endings. All of the endings in this list are attached to the stem of a True Adjective. Although Quasi and Noun + NO adjectives cannot themselves be conjugated, the same endings may be used with them by manipulating the verb **desu** or by simply adding the ending after the adjective without **desu**. *(See notes for "Q/N Adjectives" with each ending below.)*

Endings that follow the Informal Form of an adjective are presented in Chapter 18, *Informal Endings*.

-kattara   *if it were, if it is*

Ex.: **Takakattara, kaimasen.**
      If it were expensive, I wouldn't have bought it.
      Hoshikattara, sashiagemasu.
      If you want it, I will give it to you.

Idiomatic: **yokattara** = *if it's okay [with you]*

Ex.: **Yokattara, ashita denwa o shimasu.**
      If it's okay with you, I will phone tomorrow.

Q/N Adjectives: Use **dattara**.

Ex.: **Kanemochi dattara, yokatta to omoimasu.**
      I think it would be great if I were rich.

-kereba   *if it is*

Ex.: **Ashita atsukereba, oyogi ni ikimashō ka?**
       If It's hot tomorrow, shall we go swimming?

Q/N Adjectives: Use **naraba** or **de areba.**

Ex.: **Shizuka de areba, hirune ga dekiru deshō.**
       If it's quiet, you can probably take a nap.
       Byōki naraba, yasunda hō ga ii to omoimasu.
       If you're sick, it's better if you rest.

-kereba [Adj] hodo   *the more [adj] the better*

Ex.: **Kōhii wa atsukereba, atsui hodo ii to omoimasu.**
       As for coffee, the hotter the better, I think. (Lit. If the coffee is hot, hot is better . . .)

Q/N Adjectives: Use **naraba [+ particle before hodo]**

Ex.: **Benri naraba, benri na hodo ii desu.** .
       The more convenient, the better.

-kereba yokatta desu   *it would be better if it were.* Often translated "I wish it were."

Ex.: **Kōhii ga atsukereba, yokatta desu.**
       It would be better if the coffee were hot. (I wish the coffee were hot.)

Q/N Adjectives: Use **naraba.**

Ex.: **Eki ni benri naraba, yokatta desu.**
       It would be better if it were convenient to the station.

-ku   Adverb Form. *(See Chapter 27, Adverbs.)*

-kunakattara   *if it were not/was not*

Ex.: **Hoshikunakattara, sutete mo ii desu.**
       If you don't want it, it's okay to throw it away.

Q/N Adjectives: Use **de[wa]nakattara.**

Ex.: **Byōki denakattara, umi ni ikimasu.**
       If I weren't sick, I would go to the beach (ocean).

-kunakereba   *if it is not*

Ex.: **Samukunakereba, Doyōbi ni yama ni ikimasu.**
       If it is not cold, on Saturday we'll go to the mountains.

Q/N Adjectives: Use **denakereba.**

Ex.: **Kyō ga benri denakereba, ashita ni shimashō.**
       If today is not convenient, let's make it tomorrow.

-kunakute   *not being, is not [adj] but [adj].* Usually calls attention to a contrast ("not this, but that").

Ex.:   **Kore wa oishikunakute, daremo tabetakunai to omoimasu.**
This doesn't taste good (isn't tasty), and nobody wants to eat it.

Ikitakunakute, koko ni nokoritai desu.
I don't want to go; I want to remain here.

Q/N Adjectives: Use **dewanakute.**

Ex.:   **Benri dewanakute, eki kara tōi desu.**
It's not convenient; it's far from the station.

-kunakute wa ikemasen/dame desu   *must be, has to be. (Lit. if it is not [adj] it is bad/inappropriate/not okay.)*

Ex.:   **Takusan no hito ga kimasu kara, heya wa hirokunakute wa ikemasen.**
A lot of people are coming, so the room has to be big (wide).

Q/N Adjectives: Use **dewanakute wa ikemasen/dame desu.**

Ex.:   **O-kyaku-sama ga kimasu node, ima wa kirei dewanakute wa ikemasen.**
Guests are coming, so the living room has to be clean.

-kunaru   *become [adj]*

Ex.:   **Kesa hayaku atsukunarimashita, ne.**
It became hot early this morning, didn't it?
Iyahōn o tsukaeba, kikiyasukunaru to omoimasu.
If you use earphones, I think it will become easier to hear.

Idiomatic: **nakunaru** = *die; get lost*

Ex.:   **Otōsan wa kyonen nakunarimashita.**   *My father died last year.*
Okane ga nakunatte, komarimashita.
My money ran out, and I was in a bind.

Q/N Adjectives: Use **ni naru.**

Ex.:   **Hayaku genki ni natte kudasai.**   *Please get well quickly.*

-kusuru   *make [adj]*

Ex.:   **Mō chotto yasukushite kudasaimasen ka?**
Won't you make it a little cheaper?
Hon o irete, nimotsu o omotakushimashita.
I put the books in, and it made the package heavy.

Idiomatic: **nakusu** = *lose*

Ex.:   **Densha no naka de kaban o nakushimashita.**
I lost my briefcase inside the train.

Q/N Adjectives: Use **ni suru.**

Ex.: **Sensei wa tesuto o kantan ni shimashita.**
The teacher made the test simple.

Idiomatic: **kirei ni suru** = *to clean, make [something] clean*

Ex.: **Ashita heya o kirei ni shimasu.** *I will clean my room tomorrow.*

-kute TE-form of True Adjectives. Used to list two or more adjectives or to connect an adjective/verb sequence. Often indicates a mild cause/effect relationship. "And" or "and so" can be used in English translation. Past or present tense is determined by the final adjective or verb.

Ex.: **Kono apāto wa semakute kurai desu.**
This apartment is small (narrow) and dark.
Kono heya wa semakute yahari kawaritai to omoimasu.
This room is small, and so I think I would like to change, after all.
Nanika tabetakute, chikaku no pan'ya ni ikimashita.
I wanted to eat something, and so I went to a nearby bakery.

Q/N Adjectives: Use **de.**

Ex.: **Nihonshoku ga daisuki de, mainichi tabemasu.**
I love Japanese food and eat it every day.

-kutemo *even if it is*

Ex.: **Chiisakutemo daijōbu desu.** *It's okay even if it is small.*
Yominikukutemo, yomanakereba narimasen.
I have to read it, even if it is hard to read.

Q/N Adjectives: Use **demo.**

Ex.: **Byōki demo, hatarakanakute wa ikemasen.**
Even if I am sick, I have to work.

-kute tamarimasen *unbearably*

Ex.: **Kyō wa atsukute tamarimasen, ne.**
Today is unbearably hot, isn't it?
Ikitakute tamarimasen yo.
I want so much to go that I can't stand it! (Lit. I am unbearably desirous of going.)

Q/N Adjectives: Use **de tamarimasen.**

Ex.: **Kore wa fuben de tamarimasen.**
This is so inconvenient, I can't stand it.

-kute wa ikemasen/dame desu *must not/should not be (Lit. if it is [adj] it is bad/inappropriate/not okay.)*

Ex.: **Donna ni kirei demo, takakute wa ikemasen.**
No matter how pretty it is, it mustn't be expensive.

Burausu ga midori desu kara, sukāto wa aokute wa dame desu.
Since the blouse is green, the skirt shouldn't be blue.

Q/N Adjectives: Use **dewa ikemasen/dame desu.**

Ex.: **Kodomo desu kara, amari fukuzatsu dewa ikemasen.**
They're children; so it mustn't be too complicated.

-sa Refers to the quality of the adjective; makes the adjective into a noun.
(Cf. -ness, as in "goodness," "freshness," "whiteness.")

Ex.: **Bō no nagasa wa chōdo ii to omoimasu.**
I think the length of the pole is just right.

Q/N Adjectives are not very often used with this ending. The following
are among those that sometimes will be used with **-sa.**

benrisa *(convenience)*
chūjitsusa *(loyalty)*
jūyōsa *(importance)*
kanpekisa *(flawlessness, perfection)*
nigiyakasa *(liveliness, gaiety)*
nodokasa *(tranquility)*
seikakusa *(exactness, precision, accuracy)*
shinsensa *(freshness)*
shizukasa/shizukesa *(quietness, peacefulness)*

Ex.: **Sakana no shinsensa o shirabenai to wa dame desu.**
You have to test the freshness of the fish.

-sō [desu] *looks [adj]. Creates a Quasi Adjective.*

Ex.: **Kēki wa oishisō desu.** *The cake looks delicious.*
Takasō na kaban o kaimashita.
He bought an expensive-looking briefcase.

Exceptional:

ii/yoi — yosasō desu
Ex.: **Kono hon wa yosasō desu, ne.** *This book looks good, doesn't it?*

nai — nasasō desu
Ex.: **Ano hito wa okane ga nasasō desu.**
It looks like he doesn't have any money.

Q/N Adjectives: Omit **desu.**

Ex.: **Apāto wa eki ni chikakute, benrisō desu.**
*The apartment is close to the station, and so it seems to be
convenient.*
Shizukasō na kinjo desu. *It's a quiet-looking neighborhood.*

-sugiru   *too [adj]*

> Ex.: **L-saizu wa ōkisugimasu.**
>> *The "L" (large) size is too big.*
>
>> **Kaitai desu ga, takasugiru to omoimasu.**
>> *I want to buy it, but I think it's too expensive.*

Q/N Adjectives: Omit **desu.**

> Ex.: **Ano ko wa chotto genki sugiru to omoimasen ka?**
>> *Don't you think that child is a little too lively?*

27. Adverbs

A Japanese adverb is usually placed immediately before the verb, adjective, or other adverb that it modifies. There are two kinds of adverbs: those created from adjectives and those that are not.

ADVERBS MADE FROM ADJECTIVES

Adverbs are made from True Adjectives by dropping the final syllable **i** and adding **ku**:

fukai *(deep)* — **fukaku** *(deeply)*
hayai *(quick)* — **hayaku** *(quickly)*
sugoi *(great)* — **sugoku** *(greatly/very)*

Ex.: **Fukaku kangaemashita.** *I thought deeply [about it].*
Maiasa hayaku okimasu. *I get up early every morning.*
Okāsan wa sugoku ii hito desu, ne.
Your mother is a very good person, isn't she?

Adverbs are made from Quasi and Noun + NO Adjectives by addition of the particle **ni**, instead of **na** or **no**:

buji *(safe)* — **buji ni** *(safely)*
hontō *(true)* — **hontō ni** *(truly)*
jōzu *(skillful)* — **jōzu ni** *(skillfully)*

Ex.: **Buji ni kaette kite, yokatta desu.**
Thank goodness you came back safely.
Ano hito wa hontō ni yasashii desu. *That person is truly nice.*
E o jōzu ni kakimashita. *He drew the picture well (skillfully).*

Adverbs made from adjectives are sometimes used where an adjective form would be used in English. *(See also Chapter 26, Adjective Endings.)*

Ex.: **Tanaka-san wa kesa byōki ni narimashita.**
Tanaka became sick this morning.
Nagasugimasu node, mijikaku shite kudasai.
It's too long, so please make it short[er].

When **mieru** *(be visible)* or **kikoeru** *(be audible)* follows an adverb, the phrase takes on the meaning "look/appear to be" or "sound like," respectively.

Ex.: **Koko kara mukō no tatemono wa chiisaku miemasu.**
From here the buildings over there look small.
Ojiisan no koe wa wakaku kikoemasu.
Grandfather's voice sounds young.

TRUE ADVERBS

Adverbs that are not derived from adjectives may be called True Adverbs. True Adverbs do not require a particle following. Following is a list of some common True Adverbs:

amari *([not] especially)* Used with negative verb/adjective.
chotto *(a little bit)*
ichiban *(most; lit. number one)*
mada *(yet, still)*
mata *(again)*
mattaku *(absolutely)*
mō *(already)*

nakanaka *(no matter what)*
narubeku *(as . . . as possible)*
taihen *(terribly, awfully)*
totemo *(very)*
yukkuri *(slowly, leisurely)*
zenzen *(not at all)* Used with negative verb/adjective.

Ex.: **Amari kikitakunai desu.** *I don't especially want to hear [about it].*
Narubeku hayaku denwa o shite kudasai.
Please phone as early as possible.
Kinō taihen atsukatta desu, ne.
Yesterday it was terribly hot, wasn't it?
Ano hito wa zenzen utawanakatta sō desu.
I heard that person didn't sing at all.

OTHER ADVERBIAL EXPRESSIONS

There are also certain adverbial expressions that modify whole clauses or sentences. These are usually placed either immediately before or immediately after the topic.

aikawarazu   *as usual, as always*
Ex.: **Suzuki-san wa aikawarazu kōen de ranchi o tabete imasu.**
As always, Suzuki is eating lunch at the park.

dōshitemo   *by any means, for any reason*
Ex.: **Bōi wa dōshitemo chippu o torimasen deshita.**
The bellboy would not accept a tip for any reason.

kekkyoku   *after all, in the end, in the long run*
Ex.: **Kekkyoku dare ni mo wakarimasen deshita.**
It was not, in the end, understood by anyone.

mochiron   *of course*
Ex.: **Mochiron minna ni tsutaete okimasu.**
Of course, I will inform everyone.

moshikashitara   *perhaps, it may be that*
Ex.: **Kuru hazu desu ga, moshikashitara konai ka mo shiremasen.**
He is supposed to come, but he might not, for all we know.

nante [+ Adj]   *how/what (exclamatory)*
Ex.: **Nante kawaii kodomo deshō!** *What a cute child he is!*

naruhodo   *indeed, to be sure*
Ex.: **Naruhodo ii keikaku desu, ne.** *Indeed, it is a good plan, isn't it?*

sekkaku   *kindly, with much effort, at great pain*
Ex.: **Sekkaku tameta okane o tsukatte shimatte, zannen desu ne.**
      *It's a shame to use up the money you went to such great pains
      to accumulate, isn't it?*

tonikaku   *anyway*
Ex.: **Tonikaku, osoi desu kara, kaerimashō.**
      Anyway, since it's late, let's go home.

toriaezu   *for the time being*
Ex.: **Toriaezu, shachō no henji o machimashō.**
      For the time being, let's wait for the president's response.

wazawaza   *kindly, especially, going to the bother of*
Ex.: **Wazawaza koko made go-annai kudasatte, dōmo arigatō gozaimashita.**
      Thank you for going to the bother of guiding me this far.

yahari   *after all*
Ex.: **Yahari kaisha no dairinin to shite, kaigi ni shusseki shinakute wa
      narimasen.**
      *After all, as the company's representative, you must attend the
      meeting.*

ADVERBS AS NOUNS

Certain adverbs derived from True Adjectives sometimes function as nouns.

chikai – chikaku   *(vicinity)*
Ex.: **Kono chikaku ni sunde imasu.** *I live near here (in this vicinity).*
      Chikaku no sushiya de tabemashita. *We ate at a nearby sushi bar.*

tōi – tōku   *(a distance)*
Ex.: **Tōku ni wa fune ga miemashita.** *A ship was visible in the distance.*
      Tōku no machi kara kimashita. *He came from a distant town.*

ōi – ōku   *(a great number, many)*
Ex.: **Ōku no hito wa konsāto ni kimashita.**
      A great number of people came to the concert.

hayai – hayaku   *(an early time)*
osoi – osoku   *(a late time)*
Ex.: **Mainichi asa hayaku kara yoru osoku made hatarakimasu.**
      Every day I work from early morning until late at night.

28. Comparisons

[A] YORI MO [B] NO HŌ GA [Adj.] DESU.

[B] is more [Adj.] than [A].

In the above pattern A and B are the two items being compared. The two underlined elements may be given in reverse order without affecting the meaning (**[B] no hō ga [A] yori mo [Adj.] desu**). Either phrase may be used alone, with the other phrase understood. **Mo** is often omitted.

Ex.: **Banira yori mo, chokorēto no hō ga suki desu.**
I like chocolate better than vanilla.
Sukiyaki no hō ga tenpura yori [mo] oishii to omoimasu.
I think Tenpura is tastier than Sukiyaki.
Kono kōen wa tokai yori [mo] shizuka desu.
This park is more peaceful than the metropolis.

Idiomatic: **itsumo yori** = *more than usual*
nani yori = *more than anything*

COMPARING ADJECTIVES OR VERBS

When comparing adjectives or verbs, the Informal Form is used, and **no** is omitted from **no hō ga**. A verb before **hō ga** is usually in the Plain Past form (Vta).

Ex.: **Kuruma wa, chiisai hō ga benri, deshō?**
As for cars, small ones are more convenient, aren't they?
Ano ko wa oniisan yori [mo] sei ga takai desu.
That child is taller than his older brother.
Yameta hō ga ii deshō. *It would probably be better to quit.*
Yameru yori mo, matta hō ga ii to omoimasu.
I think it's better to wait than to quit.

OTHER COMPARISON WORDS

motto *(more)*
Ex.: **Danchi wa takai desu ga, kono tatemono wa motto takai desu.**
The apartment building is tall, but this building is taller.

mottomo, ichiban *(most)*
Ex.: **Ano tatemono wa mottomo takai desu. (or ... ichiban takai desu.)**
That building yonder is tallest.

-ichi   *([number] one)*   After a word referring to a specific area, this indicates "the best in" that area.

Ex.:   **Momotarō wa "Nippon-ichi" to yobaremashita.**
Momotaro was called "the best in Japan."
Kore wa sekai-ichi no sushiya desu.
This is the best sushi restaurant in the world.

yori [+ Adj]   *(more [Adj])*

Ex.:   **Yoriyasui mono ga hoshii to omoimasu**
I think I would like a cheaper one.
Yoriyoi ningen ni naritai desu.
I want to become a better person (human being).

ma [+ Adj]   *(completely/exactly/perfectly/intensely [Adj])*   The first consonant of the adjective is usually doubled.

ma + shiro = masshiro   *(completely white)*
ma + kuro = makkuro   *(completely black)*
ma + aka = makka   *(completely red)*
ma + naka = mannaka   *(the very center)*
ma + sugu = massugu   *(perfectly straight, straight ahead)*
Exception: **ma + ao = massao**   *(deep blue)*

Ex.:   **Ano hito no kami wa makkuro desu, ne.**
That person's hair is completely black, isn't it?
Shikaku no mannaka ni namae ga kaite arimashita.
In the very center of the square, a name was written.
Massugu itte kudasai.   *Please go straight ahead.*

29. Noun Expressions

Following is a selection of common expressions that follow and modify nouns.

bakari, dake   *only.* **Bakari** replaces **ga** or **o**; both **bakari** and **dake** usually replace **wa**. Other particles may be placed either before or after either **bakari** or **dake**.

> Ex.: **Ue no tana ni wa jisho bakari oite arimasu.**
> *On the top shelf only dictionaries have been placed.*
> **Ringo dake [o] kaimashita.** *I bought only apples.*
> **Sensei dake ni kiita no desu.** (or **Sensei ni dake ...**)
> *I asked only the teacher.*

bakari/dake de naku   *not only*

> Ex.: **Hana bakari de naku, kabin mo utte imasu.**
> *They are selling not only flowers, but vases as well.*
> **Yōfuku dake de naku, kutsu mo hitsuyō desu.**
> *I need not only clothes, but shoes as well.*

demo   *even.* Replaces **wa, ga,** and any other particle that is not needed for clarification.

> Ex.: **Shachō-san demo ikimashita.**
> *Even the company president went.*
> **Ano ko wa muzukashii koto demo yatte mimasu.**
> *That child tries even hard things.*

hodo   *as [much] as.* After a noun, this expression is followed by a negative verb or adjective.

> Ex.: **Naoko hodo jōzu dewa arimasen.**
> *I am not as good [at it] as Naoko.*

After a counter, **hodo** means "about" or "approximately" and can be followed by either negative or positive verb/adjective.

> Ex.: **Kōra o sanbon hodo nomimashita.**
> *I drank about three bottles of Cola.*

-jō   *from the standpoint of*

> Ex.: **Rekishijō no jūyōsa o kangaete okimashō.**
> *Let's consider its historical importance. (Lit. ... importance from the standpoint of history.)*

-kusai   *smell of*

> Ex.: **Daidokoro wa sakanakusai desu.** *The kitchen smells of fish.*

mitai/rashii [desu] *look like, appear to be, [Noun]-like*

Ex.: **Oisha-san wa gaijin mitai desu.** *The doctor looks like a foreigner.*
Suzuki-san no shujin wa totemo otokorashii hito desu.
Mrs. Suzuki's husband is a very manly person.

nante *such [things] as*

Ex.: **Konpyūtā nante wakaranai no desu.**
I don't understand [such things as] computers.

nashi [de] *without*

Ex.: **Sētā nashi de dekakete shimaimashita.**
I went out without a sweater.

ni kansuru/kanshite, ni taisuru/taishite, ni tsuite *concerning, about*

Ex.: **Suzuki-san wa Nihon no rekishi ni kanshite hanashimashita.**
Suzuki spoke about Japanese history.
Keizai ni taisuru hōkokusho wa mada yonde imasen.
I have not yet read the report concerning economics.
Shiken no kekka ni tsuite, sensei ni kiite kudasai.
Please ask the teacher about the results of the exam.

ni ki ga tsuku *notice, take notice of*

Ex.: **Totemo suki datta node, nedan ni ki ga tsukimasen deshita.**
Because I liked it a lot, I didn't notice the price.

ni ki o tsukeru *pay attention to, be careful of, watch [out for]*

Ex.: **Ashimoto ni ki o tsukete kudasai.**
*Please watch your step. (Lit. . . . be careful of the area
at your feet.)*

ni okeru *in, at, on [a specified area]*

Ex.: **Nihon ni okeru mottomo yūmei na kashu desu.**
He is the most famous singer in Japan.

ni suru *decide on*

Ex.: **Nomimono wa, aisukōhii ni shimasu.**
*As for something to drink, I'll make it iced coffee. (Lit. I'll
decide on iced coffee.)*

ni taishite, ni tsuite *(See* **ni kansuru.***)*

ni totte *[as] for, from the standpoint of*

Ex.: **Watakushi ni totte, gorufu wa ichiban tanoshii desu.**
For me, golf is the most fun.

ni yotte *through, by way of, by means of, depending on*

Ex.: **Minna no kyōryoku ni yotte dekimashita.**
Through the cooperation of everyone, we were able to do it.

Shinbun ni yotte, sekai no dekigoto o naraimasu.
We learn the things of the world by way of the newspaper.
Hito ni yotte chigaimasu.   *It differs, depending on the person.*

no kawari [ni]   *instead of, in place of*

Ex.: Jitensha no kawari ni ōtobai o karimashita.
I borrowed a motorcycle instead of a bike.
Otōsan no kawari ni oniisan ga itte mo ii desu.
Your older brother may go in place of your father.

no koto   *about (Lit. things of)*

Ex.: Kyō ichinichijū onēsan no koto o kangaete imashita.
I was thinking about my older sister all day today.
Dansei no koto ga wakaranai no desu.
I don't understand [things about] men.

no naka/uchi   *among, [with] in*

Ex.: Kore no naka kara hitotsu erande kudasai.
Please choose one from among these.
Nihon no sakka no uchi, Sōseki ga ichiban suki desu.
Among Japan's writers, I like Soseki best.

no tame ni   *for, in behalf of, for the sake of; because of*

Ex.: Okane no tame ni hataraite imasu.   *I am working for the money.*
Suzuki-san wa minna no tame ni tsukurimashita.
Suzuki made them for everybody.
Byōki no tame ni yasumimashita.
I took the day off (rested) because of illness.

no uchi   *(See no naka.)*

no ue [ni]   *in addition to, on top of*

Ex.: Byōki no ue ni, iroiro na mondai ga aru mitai desu.
He appears to have various problems in addition to his illness.

no yō [ni]   *like.* Without *ni*, this creates a Quasi Adjective phrase.

Ex.: Oniisan no yō ni, mainichi undō shinakute wa narimasen.
I need to exercise every day, like older brother.
Sensei no yō na hito ni naritai desu.
I want to become a person like [my] teacher.

o moto ni shite   *based on*

Ex.: Kana wa kanji o moto ni shite tsukurareta sō desu.
I heard that kana is based on kanji.

o tōshite   *through, with/by means of, by way of*

Ex.: Tomodachi o tōshite, Suzuki-san ni aimashita.
I met Suzuki through a friend.

shika   *[nothing/anything] except.* Used with negative verb/adjective.
Shika replaces **wa, ga,** or **o.** Other particles may be placed before **shika,** as appropriate.

Ex.:   **Ringo shika kaimasen deshita.** *I didn't buy anything but apples.*
Basu de shika ikenai to omoimasu.
I think you can't get (go) there except by bus.
Suzuki-san ni shika kikanakatta desu.
I didn't ask anybody but Suzuki.

-teki   *-like, -ish, having the qualities of; -ical, -ically*

Ex.:   **Yukiko wa totemo josei-teki na hito desu.**
Yukiko is a very feminine person.
Rekishi-teki ni daiji na dekigoto desu.
It is a historically important event.

to chigatte   *unlike, differing from*

Ex.:   **Suzuki-san to chigatte, Takagi-sensei wa itsumo teinei desu.**
Unlike Suzuki, Professor Takagi is always polite.

to iu   *called, so-called*

Ex.:   **Sumisu to iu hito kara denwa ga kakatte kimashita.**
A phone call came from a person called "Smith."
Mitsukoshi to iu depāto de kaimashita.
I bought it at a department store called "Mitsukoshi."

to iu yō [na]   *such [things] as, like*

Ex.:   **Hōseki to iu yō na mono wa takasugiru to omoimasu.**
I think such things as jewels (jewelry) are too expensive.

to shite   *as, in the capacity of*

Ex.:   **Kaisha no daihyōsha to shite itte kimashita.**
I went as a representative of the company.
Tōkyō de eigo no kyōshi to shite hataraite imasu.
He is working in Tokyo in the capacity of an English teacher.

to tomo ni   *[along] with, in the company of*

Ex.:   **Sūgaku to tomo ni, rekishi mo kokugo mo benkyō shimasu.**
Along with math, they study both history and language.
Yukiko wa tomodachi to tomo ni haitte kimashita.
Yukiko came in, in the company of her friend.

30. Compound Nouns

Many compound nouns are created by combining nouns with other nouns, with adjectives, and with noun forms of verbs. The resulting compound is then treated like any other noun.

When a verb is used in a compound, it is used in the V2 form. A True Adjective will be reduced to its stem.

If the second part of the compound begins with an unvoiced consonant (k, s, sh, t, ch, h, f, p), it will sometimes be changed to a voiced consonant (g, z, j, d, b).

Following is a selection of common compound nouns.

ami *(net)* + **to** *(door)* = **amido** *(screen door)*

asa *(morning)* + **hi** *(sun)* = **asahi** *(morning sun)*

deru *(to exit)* + **hairu** *(to enter)* = **dehairi** *(going in and out)*

deru *(to exit)* + **kuchi** *(mouth)* = **deguchi** *(exit)*

furui *(old)* + **hon** *(book)* = **furuhon** *(second-hand books)*

ha *(tooth)* + **migaku** *(to polish)* = **hamigaki** *(toothpaste)*

hana *(nose)* + **chi** *(blood)* = **hanaji** *(nosebleed)*

hana *(flower)* + **miru** *(to see)* = **hanami** *(flower-viewing)*

hayai *(early)* + **okiru** *(to get up, wake up)* = **hayaoki** *(early riser)*

hiru *(noon)* + **neru** *(to sleep)* = **hirune** *(nap, siesta)*

hito *(person)* + **korosu** *(to kill)* = **hitogoroshi** *(homicide)*

kesu *(to erase)* + **gomu** *(rubber)* = **keshigomu** *(eraser)*

yama *(mountain)* + **noboru** *(to climb)* = **yamanobori** *(mountain climbing)*

Many Japanese family and place names are compounds of common words, such as the following.

hiroi *(wide)* + **shima** *(island)* = **Hiroshima**

hoshi *(star)* + **no** *(field)* = **Hoshino**

mizu *(water)* + **tani** *(valley)* = **Mizutani**

mori *(grove)* + **kuchi** *(mouth, entrance)* = **Moriguchi**

oka *(hill)* + **moto** *(base)* = **Okamoto**

ta *(rice paddy)* + **naka** *(center)* = **Tanaka**

takai *(high)* + **yama** *(mountain)* = **Takayama**

31. Common Noun Prefixes & Suffixes

Prefix/Suffix	Meaning/Reference	Example
bei-, -bei	American (U.S.)	Beikoku *(U.S.A.)* Nichibei *(Japan-U.S. [relations])*
chū-, -chū/-jū	center; during, entire [period]	chūshin *(center, core)* gozenchū *(in the morning)* hitobanjū *(all night long)*
dai-	number, order	daiichi *(number one, best)*
dai-/tai-	great, large	daigaku *(university)* taishi *(ambassador)*
-dama	coin	jūen-dama *(10-yen coin)*
dan-, -dan	group, party	danchō *(group leader)* daihyōdan *(representative party)*
dō-	same	dōji [ni] *([at] the same time)* dōfū [suru] *(enclose [in envelope])*
-dō	hall, location; shop	shokudō *(cafeteria)* Fūgetsu-dō *(Fugetsu store)*
ei-, -ei	England, English	Eiryō *(British territory)* waei *(Japanese-English [dictionary])*
fu-	dis-, in-, un-	fusoku *(insufficient)* fukigen *(cross, grouchy)*
fuku-	sub-, vice-	fuku-kaichō *(vice-chairman)* fuku-daitōryō *(vice-president)*
-go	language	Nihongo *(Japanese language)* keigo *(honorific language)*
han-	anti-, against	hanbei *(anti-American)* hantai *(opposite)*
han-	half, semi-	hanbun *(a half portion)* hanseiki *(half a century)*
-hatsu	departure	Kōbe-hatsu *(departing Kobe)* niji-hatsu *(2:00 departure)*
hon-	this, the same	honjitsu *(this day)* honnin *(he, himself)*
-iri	including, inserting	tamago-iri *(with egg)* tamanegi-iri *(with onions)*
-jin	person, nationality	Nihonjin *(Japanese person)*
-kai	meeting, group	taikai *(conference, convention)* bōnenkai *(year-end party)*
-ke	family	Suzuki-ke *(Suzuki family)*
ko-	petty, small	koneko *(kitten)* kobito *(dwarf, little person)*
kon-	this	kondo *(this time, this round)* konnichi *(this day)*
kyū-, -kyū	quick, sudden	kyūkō *(express [train])* tokkyū *(special express [train])*
kyū-	rest, absence	kyūjitsu *(holiday)* kyūkei *(rest, break, recess)*
mai-	every	maido *(every time)* mainen *(every year)*

Prefix/Suffix	Meaning/Reference	Example
mei-	famous, noted	meibutsu *(famous wares)*
		meimon *(noted group/family)*
mu-	non-, without	muri *(unreasonable, impossible)*
		muryō *(free of charge)*
sai-	the most	saikō *(greatest)*
		saisho *(first)*, saigo *(last)*
-satsu	bill (money)	ichiman'ensatsu *(one-MAN bill)*
		sen'ensatsu *(thousand-yen bill)*
-sei	source, origin	Nihon-sei *(made in Japan)*
-sen	transit line	Hibiya-sen *(Hibiya Line)*
-sho/-jo	place location	shiyakusho *(city government office)*
		teiryūjo *(bus stop)*
-shu	agent, operator,	untenshu *(driver)*
	person	kashu *(singer)*
sū-	several, so many	sūjitsu *(several days)*
		sūhyaku *(several hundred)*
tō-	the one in question,	tōjitsu *(the day in question)*
	the said	tōnin *(the said person)*
-tsuki	including, with	kagu-tsuki *(furnished)*
		sarada-tsuki *(with salad)*
wa-, -wa	Japanese [style]	washoku *(Japanese food)*
		wafuku *(Japanese-style clothing)*
		eiwa *(English-Japanese [dictionary])*
-ya	shop, dealer	pan'ya *(bakery, bread store)*
		hanaya-san *(florist)*
yō-	Western [style]	yōfuku *(Western-style clothing)*
		yōshoku *(Western meal/food)*
-yuki	destination	higashi-yuki *(eastbound)*
		Ōta-yuki *(bound for Ota)*
zen-	complete, whole	zenkoku *(the whole country)*
		zensekai *(the whole world)*
		zenbu *(everything, all)*

32. Relative Clauses

A relative clause is a clause that describes a noun. In English the relative clause comes after the noun it describes; for example, "the person who came to the office," "the place where we first met," "the thing that I wanted to tell you," etc.

In Japanese a relative clause is placed *before* the noun it describes. The verb of the descriptive clause is usually in an Informal Form. This is similar to the creation of a noun clause by adding **koto** after the Informal Form of a verb. *(See Chapter 18, Informal Endings: KOTO.)*

Ex.: **Kesa jimusho ni kita hito wa dare desu ka?**
Who is the person who came to the office this morning?
Ashita iku tokoro wa amari tōkunai desu.
The place where [we] are going tomorrow is not very far.
Yūbe yonde ita shinbun wa [ima] doko desu ka?
Where is the newspaper [that] I was reading last night?

DESU IN RELATIVE CLAUSES

Da and **datta** (Informal present and past tense of **desu**) are not used in front of a noun in the Normal-polite level. **Dearu** and **deatta** are possible but are used primarily to emphasize a contrast.

Ex.: **Gaijin dearu hito** = *people who are foreigners*
(as opposed to people who are not foreigners)
Sensei deatta hito = *people who were (had been) teachers*
(as opposed to people who were not teachers)

SUBJECT OF A RELATIVE CLAUSE

When the subject of the relative clause is stated, if it is different from the subject of the main clause, the preferred particle is **ga** or **no**, rather than **wa**. *(See also Chapter 21, Particles: GA.)*

Ex.: **Onēsan no yonde iru hon wa rekishi no hon desu.**
The book that older sister is reading is a history book.
Yukiko ga kaita tegami wa mō dashita no desu ka?
Did you already mail the letter that Yukiko wrote?

33. Relative Positions

Position words in English are usually considered adverbs; in Japanese they act as nouns. The basic pattern for telling the location of one item in relation to another is:

[A] WA [B] NO [Position] NI / DE [Verb]

In this pattern A is the item in question; B is the item it is placed in relation to. *(See below for example sentences.)*

EXPRESSING POSITION WITH <u>KO-SO-A-DO</u>

Koko, soko, asoko/mukō and **doko** *(here, there, over there, where?)* were introduced in Chapter 20, *Demonstrative Forms.* When the verb is **desu**, these words do not require a particle; with any other verb, however, an appropriate particle must be used.

Ex.: **Pen wa koko desu.** *The pen is here.*
Pen wa koko ni arimasu. *The pen is here.*
Sensei wa asoko ni imasu. *The teacher is over there.*
Kodomo wa mukō kara hashitte kimashita.
The child came running from over there.
Ano hito wa asoko de hataraite imasu.
That person is working over there.

POSITION WORDS

Following is a selection of common position words.

aida *(area between two points in time or space)*	**mukō** *(other side/beyond)*
	naka *(inside)*
chikaku *(nearby area)*	**nishi** *(west)*
hidari *(left)*	**soba** *(nearby area/vicinity)*
higashi *(east)*	**soto** *(outside)*
kita *(north)*	**tonari** *(neighboring area)*
mae *(front)*	**ue** *(top/upper portion)*
mawari *(surrounding area)*	**ura** *(back side/rear face)*
migi *(right)*	**ushiro** *(rear area/behind)*
minami *(south)*	**yoko** *(lateral area/side)*

POSITION WORDS WITH EXISTENCE VERBS

The particle used when telling where something *exists* or *is located* is **ni**.
There are relatively few verbs that indicate existence or location; they include **aru** and **iru** *(be located)*, **oku** *(put [down], place)*, **saku** *(bloom)*,

sumu *(reside, live in a place)*, **suwaru** *(sit/sit down)*, **tatsu** *(stand/stand up)*,
tomaru *(stop over, stay [overnight])*.

Ex.: **Kare wa toshokan no naka ni imasu.** *He is inside the library.*
Saifu wa tsukue no ue ni arimasu. *The wallet is on top of the desk.*
Hon o tansu no ue ni okimashita.
I put the book on top of the dresser.
Niwa ni hana ga saite imasu. *Flowers are blooming in the garden.*
Eki no chikaku ni sunde imasu. *I live near the station.*
Michio-kun wa watashi no tonari ni suwatte imasu.
Michio is sitting next to me.
Tanaka-san wa doa no migi ni tatte imasu.
Tanaka is standing to the right of the door.
Hawai ni iku toki hoteru ni tomarimasu ka?
When you go to Hawaii, will you stay in a hotel?

POSITION WORDS WITH ACTION VERBS

The particle used when telling where an action takes place is **de**. Generally,
verbs that are not existence verbs *(see above)* or motion verbs *(go, come,
return, etc.)* are action verbs.

Ex.: **Kanojo wa ginkō no chikaku de hatarakimasu.**
She works near the bank.
Kodomo-tachi wa michi no mukō de asonde imasu.
The children are playing on the other side of the street.
Rokuji made eki no mae de machimashita.
I waited in front of the station until 6:00.
Mainichi toshokan de benkyō shimasu.
I study at the library every day.
Okāsan wa daidokoro de ryōri o tsukutte imasu.
Mother is in the kitchen cooking.

SPECIAL EXPRESSIONS

The following special expressions are used to indicate position relative to
time, space, or concept. When acting as adverbs, they may be followed by
ni or no particle; when acting as adjectives, they are followed by **no**; when
acting as nouns, they are followed by **wa** or some other appropriate particle.

igai   *outside, other than, besides, in addition, except*

Ex.: **Kazoku igai ni tomodachi ga imasen.**
I have no friends besides my family.
Kazoku igai no tomodachi wa sukunai desu.
Friends outside my family are few.

igo   *after, following*

Ex.:   **Doyōbi igo [wa] jikan ga aru deshō.**
I will probably have time after Saturday.
Doyōbi igo no hima na toki ni shimashō.
Let's do it in our spare time after Saturday.

ijō   *over, above, beyond, more than, further; the above-mentioned, the following*

Ex.:   **Sore ijō iu koto wa arimasen.**   *I have nothing to say beyond that.*
Ijō no setsumei de fusoku naraba, sensei ni tazunete kudasai.
If the foregoing explanation is insufficient, please inquire of the instructor.

Idiomatic: **Ijō desu.**   *That's all. / The end. / Concluded.*

ika   *below, less than, under; the following, the below-mentioned*

Ex.:   **Nedan ga ichiman-en ika ni nareba kaimasu.**
When the price drops (becomes) below 10,000 yen, I will buy it.
Gosai ika no kodomo wa haitte wa ikenai sō desu.
I hear that children under five are not allowed to enter.

ikō   *on and after, since, afterward*

Ex.:   **Jūgatsu ikō soko de hataraite imasu.**
I have been working there since October.
Kyonen ikō no shigoto wa muzukashikunarimashita.
My work since last year has become more difficult.

izen   *before, prior to, ago, on a previous occasion*

Ex.:   **Izen Hawai ni sunde ita no desu.**   *I lived in Hawaii before.*
Gogatsu izen no koto deshita.
It was something that happened before May.
Watakushi-tachi wa izen kara no shiriai desu.
We are acquaintances from before (for some time).

POSITION WORDS AS ADJECTIVES

Any position word, including **ko-so-a-do**, can be used to describe a noun by placing it in front of the noun, with the particle **no** following the position word.

Ex.:   **Asoko no kuruma wa watakushi no desu.**   *The car over there is mine.*
Tonari no biru wa yūbinkyoku desu.
The neighboring building is the post office.
Watakushi no mawari no hito wa minna shinseki desu.
The people around me are all relatives.

34. Asking & Giving Directions

In addition to relative position words presented in the previous chapter, the following expressions are useful for asking and giving directions.

kado *(corner)*
kaidan *(stairway)*
kōsoku dōro *(highway, freeway)*
massugu *(straight [ahead])*
magaru *(turn)*
michi *(street, path)*
mukau *(to face [a direction])*
noboru *(climb, ascend, embark)*
ōdanhodō *(crosswalk)*

oriru *(descend, disembark)*
shingō *(traffic signal)*
tōri, dōri *(street, roadway)*
tōru *(pass along/through)*
tsukiataru *(to come to a dead-end or T-intersection)*
tsuzuku *(to continue)*
wataru *(to cross/pass over)*

____ wa dochira desu ka? *In which direction is ____?*
____ wa doko desu ka? *Where is ____?*
Dono yō ni ikeba ii desu ka? *How can I get there?*
Dochira e ikeba ii desu ka? *Which way do I go?*
[Massugu] itte kudasai. *Please go [straight ahead].*
[Migi] ni magatte kudasai. *Please turn to the [right].*
[Ginkō no mae] de tomatte kudasai. *Please stop [in front of the bank].*
Chizu o kaite kudasaimasen ka? *Won't you please draw me a map?*
Jūsho o oshiete kudasai. *Please tell me the address.*

PARTICLE O WITH DIRECTIONS

The particle for turning a corner, crossing a street, walking a certain path, etc., is **o**, as in **eki o deru** *(exit/leave the station)*, **kado o magaru** *(turn the corner)*, **shingō o migi ni magaru** *(turn right at the traffic signal)*, **hashi o wataru** *(cross the bridge)*, **michi o aruku** *(walk [along] a street)*.

Ex.: **Eki o dete kara, migi ni magatte shingō made ikimasu. Yūbinkyoku wa sono hidari ni arimasu.**

After leaving the station, turn right and go as far as the traffic signal. The post office is on the left.

Kono mae no michi o massugu gojū mētoru gurai iku to, tsukiatari-masu. Soko o mata migi ni chotto dake aruku to, pan'ya ga arimasu. Posuto wa sono mukō desu.

If you go straight about 50 meters along the road out front, it comes to a T-intersection. If you walk to the right again for a short distance you will see a bakery. The mailbox is beyond that.

35. Idiomatic Characteristics of Some Common Words

ARU / IRU / DESU

All three of these verbs are translated "to be" in English, but each has its own specific meaning.

Desu is explained in detail in Chapter 5.

Aru and **iru** both mean "exist" or "be located," but the subject of **iru** must be either a person or an animal, while the subject of **aru** must be anything else.

> Ex.: **Sensei wa kyōshitsu ni imasu.** *The teacher is in the classroom.*
> **Kōen ni wa iroiro na tori ga imasu.**
> *In the park there are various [kinds of] birds.*
> **Pen wa tēburu no ue ni arimasu.** *The pen is on top of the table.*
> **Hako no naka ni wa takusan no mono ga arimasu.**
> *Inside the box there are lots of things.*

ARU/IRU vs. MOTSU and KAU

Aru is used idiomatically where "to have" would be used in English, when the item in possession is not a person or an animal. The English subject becomes the Japanese topic (followed by **wa**), and the English direct object (the item in possession) becomes the Japanese subject (followed by **ga**).

> Ex.: **Watakushi wa enpitsu ga arimasu.**
> *I have a pencil. (Lit. As for me, a pencil exists/is located.)*

In most cases where **aru** is used in this sense, **motsu** *(own, possess)* is also appropriate, and it is usually used in the Progressive Form (action in progress). With **motsu**, however, the meaning "to have" is more literal, and the direct object particle **o** follows the item in possession. The English subject is both the topic and subject of the Japanese version of the sentence.

> Ex.: **Watakushi wa enpitsu o motte imasu.**
> *I have (am holding/possess) a pencil.*

When the "item" in possession is a person, usually **iru** will be used, although in some cases **desu** is appropriate. **Motsu** is never used to refer to people.

> Ex.: **O-kosan wa nannin imasu ka?** / **O-kosan wa nannin desu ka?**
> *How many children do you have? / [As for you] how many children are there?*

When the thing possessed is an animal, **iru** may be used, but more often the verb **kau** *(keep, raise, rear, feed)* is appropriate.

Ex.: **Inu o sanbiki katte imasu.** *I have (am raising) three dogs.*

CHOTTO

Literally meaning "a little" or "a little bit," this word is often used to deny a request or express a negative viewpoint or response. It may be followed by an apology or excuse, or the apology may be left to the listener's understanding.

Ex.: A: **Issho ni ikimasen ka?**
　　 B: **Chotto [sumimasen], ne.**
　　　 A: Won't you come with us?
　　　 B: I'm sorry, no. (Lit. Excuse me a little bit.)

　　 A: **Are wa totemo omoshiroi eiga deshita, ne?**
　　 B: **Maa, chotto . . .**
　　　 A: That was a really funny movie, wasn't it?
　　　 B: Well, [maybe] a little.

DŌMO

An intensifier that is often translated "very" or "very much," **dōmo** is also used as a casual, abbreviated version of a number of polite phrases, such as **[dōmo] arigatō gozaimasu, [dōmo] sumimasen, [dōmo] shitsurei shimasu,** etc. Context usually makes it clear what meaning is intended.

KURU

In English "come" is often used when the intended destination is the place where the listener is or will be, or some place that pertains to the listener, as in "I'm coming to your house on Saturday."

In Japanese, however, **kuru** *(come)* is used only when the speaker is at the destination referred to. Therefore, a sentence such as **Ashita kimasu** *(I'm coming tomorrow)* would be appropriate only if the speaker is in the place where he again intends to come. Otherwise, **iku** *(go)* is used.

MŌ

Mō usually means "already," but before a word that refers to an amount or quantity, it takes the meaning "more" or "another."

Ex.: **Mō ichido itte kudasai.** *Please say it one more time.*
　　 Mō sukoshi itadakimasu. *I'll have (partake of) a little more.*
　　 Mō ippai, o-negai shimasu. *One more cup, please.*
　　 Mō hitotsu kaimashō. *Let's buy another one.*

With a negative verb or adjective, **mō** can mean "[not] any more."

Ex.: **Mō konai desu.** *He won't come any more.*
Mō wakakunai desu. *I'm not young any more.*

Idiomatic: **Mō ii desu.** *That's enough.*

Mō by itself is often used as an expression of disgust or offense. Usually it will be drawn out in low tones.

Ex.: **A: Chotto futotte irun' desu ne, onēsan.** *(Casual)*
B: Mō . . . Shitsurei!
A: You're a little overweight, aren't you, young woman?
B: Well . . . How rude!

SHIRU

In the Normal-polite level of speech, the present positive form of the verb **shiru** (**shirimasu**) is never used; it is always replaced by the Progressive form **shitte imasu**. Informal and other forms are not affected.

Ex.: **Ano hito o shitte imasu ka?** *Do you know that person?*
Iie, shirimasen. *No, I don't know [him].)*

SUKI DESU

Although the phrase **[Anata ga] suki desu** may be literally translated "I like you," it has a stronger romantic meaning than the English phrase indicates. It may be legitimately translated "I love you" in most cases.

SURU

The verb **suru** *(do)* has many special uses that do not translate exactly into English. Following are examples of uses that are not covered in other parts of this book.

wear/grow – physical characteristics

Ex.: **Ano hito wa kami o nagaku shite imasu.**
That person is wearing/growing his hair long.

play – sports, games

Ex.: **Nanika supōtsu o shimasu ka?** *Do you play any kind of sports?*
Toranpu o shimashō ka? *Shall we play cards?*

feel, be, act – emotions, feelings, temporary mental state

Ex.: **Kyō chotto iraira shite imasu.** *I am a little bit irritable today.*
Tsukaremashita kara, bon'yari shite imashita.
I was [being] absent-minded (daydreaming) because I was tired.

get/incur — injury

Ex.: **Kinō jitensha no jiko de kega o shimashita.**
    Yesterday I injured myself in a bicycle accident.

make, have — form, shape, sound, smell, taste, color, feel

Ex.: **Ano ko wa jōbu na karada o shite imasu, ne.**
    That child has a healthy body, doesn't he?
    Mado wa marui katachi o shite imasu.
    The window has a round shape.
    Ayashii oto ga shimashita.
    It made a suspicious noise.
    Kēki wa ii nioi ga shite imasu.
    The cake smells good (has a good smell).
    Ichigo no aji ga shite imasu.
    It tastes (has a taste) like strawberries.
    Kono kuruma wa hen na iro o shite imasu.
    This car has a strange color.
    Chotto hen na kimochi ga shimasu.
    It feels a little strange.

wear, put on — small pieces of clothing or jewelry

Ex.: **Otōsan wa itsumo nekutai o shimasu.**
    Father always wears a necktie.
    Kin'iro no burōchi o shite imashita.
    I was wearing a gold brooch.

WAKARU

Although this word means "understand" or "be understood," it is often used where "know" would be used in English.

Ex.: **A: Kurasu wa nanji kara hajimarimasu ka?**
    B: Wakarimasen.
    A: What time does the class begin?
    B: I don't know. (Lit. I don't understand.)

36. Transitive & Intransitive Pairs

Transitive verbs are those that act on a direct object; for example, "hit," "throw," and "give" are all transitive verbs because you can hit *something,* throw *something,* and give *something.*

Intransitive verbs cannot take a direct object. You cannot "go" *something* or "come" *something,* so those verbs are intransitive.

Some verbs can be used either way; "play," for example, can be transitive *(play the piano, play a game)* or intransitive *(play in the yard, play with a friend).*

In Japanese many transitive verbs have an intransitive counterpart. Following is a selection of common transitive/intransitive pairs.

Transitive	Intransitive
ageru *(raise)*	**agaru** *(rise, ascend)*
akeru *(open [something])*	**aku** *(open up)*
atsumeru *(gather [things])*	**atsumaru** *(gather [together])*
dasu *(send [out])*	**deru** *(go out exit)*
hajimeru *(begin [something])*	**hajimaru** *[begin)*
hiyasu *(make [something] cold)*	**hieru** *(get cold)*
kaesu *(return [something])*	**kaeru** *(return, go back)*
kimeru *(decide [something])*	**kimaru** *(be decided)*
kowasu *(break [something])*	**kowareru** *(break [up])*
mawasu *(turn [something])*	**mawaru** *(turn [around])*
naosu *(fix [something])*	**naoru** *(heal)*
noseru *(put on)*	**noru** *(get on)*
okosu *(wake [someone] up)*	**okiru** *(wake up)*
otosu *(drop [something])*	**ochiru** *(fall)*
shimeru *(fasten [something])*	**shimaru** *(close up)*
tateru *(set [something] up)*	**tatsu** *(stand up)*
todokeru *(deliver [something])*	**todoku** *(reach, arrive)*

Ex.: **Hata o agemashita.** *I raised the flag.*
Fūsen wa agarimashita. *The balloon ascended.*
Kurasu o hajimemashō. *Let's begin the class.*
Kurasu wa sorosoro hajimarimasu. *The class will begin shortly.*
Tokei o kowashimashita. *I broke the clock.*
Tokei wa kowaremashita. *The clock broke.*
Kutsu o naoshite kudasai. *Please repair the shoes.*
Hayaku naotte kudasai. *Please get well quickly.*

Idiomatic: **Deru** makes a direct object of the place being exited.

Ex.: **Heya o dete kudasai.** *Please leave the room.*

37. Honorifics

The concept of Honorifics has evolved over the centuries as part of the Japanese tradition of courtesy and protocol. Honorific words, phrases, and expressions are used by the speaker to show respect to the person he is addressing, always putting that person on a higher plane than himself; that is, anything that belongs to "me" is abased, while anything that belongs to "you" is exalted. Following is a basic overview of Honorific speech.

PREFIXES

Among Honorific expressions are certain prefixes and suffixes that have no inherent meaning but simply indicate respect or courtesy. The most common Honorific prefixes are **o-** and **go-**, as in the following examples:

namae *(name, my name)*	**shujin** *(husband, my husband)*
o-namae *(your name)*	**go-shujin** *(your husband)*

Certain words are traditionally preceded by an Honorific prefix, even though they may not clearly pertain to either the speaker or anyone else, such as **ocha** *(tea)* and **gohan** *(cooked rice)*. Honorific prefixes are also used with certain polite or idiomatic phrases, such as **Yoroshiku o-negai shimasu** *(Please accept my regards)* and **Go-kigen yo** *(Good luck)*.

The choice of **o-** or **go-** is primarily dictated by tradition, although personal preference is occasionally involved. Generally speaking, **go-** is a stronger (more polite/respectful) Honorific than **o-**.

SUFFIXES

Suffixes **-san** and **-sama** are added to the name or title of the person being addressed or referred to. They should *never* be added to one's own name.

-Sama is a somewhat stronger Honorific than **-san**. Neither suffix indicates gender or marital status, although they are often translated into English as "Mr.," "Mrs.," "Miss," or "Ms." Thus, **Tanaka-san** could be male or female, married or single. For the sake of simplicity, in this text Honorific suffixes are not translated unless context dictates otherwise.

PRONOUNS

The words **kochira**, **sochira**, and **achira** are often used to refer to *I/me, you,* and *he/him/she/her*, respectively, adding a more Honorific flavor. **Ano kata** is a polite reference to a third person **(ano hito)**. **Donata** *(who?)* is the Honorific counterpart of **dare**. *(See Chapter 23, Interrogatives.)*

VERBS

The concept of Honorifics also includes a diverse collection of verbs and other expressions that indicate a certain point of view, with respect to the speaker's social relationship with the listener or person referred to.

Humble   Humble verbs require that the speaker or a member of his own family or group be the subject.

Neutral   Neutral verbs make no requirement as to who is the subject. These are the verbs of choice in ordinary daily conversation on both the Informal and the Normal-polite level, except in certain phrases where Honorific verbs are traditionally used.

Exalted   Exalted verbs require that the subject be someone other than the speaker or a member of his family or group.

Humble and Exalted verbs are referred to collectively as Honorific verbs. Following are some common neutral verbs with their Honorific counterparts. In each case the Masu Form is given first, then the Dictionary Form of the same verb, for reference purposes. Note that the Masu Form of the starred verbs follows the syllable **i,** rather than the usual Base 2 form **ri (kudasaimasu,** not *kudasarimasu.*

| | ———————— Honorific ———————— | |
Neutral	Humble	Exalted
desu / dearu *(be, equal)*	**de gozaimasu*** **de gozaru**	**de gozaimasu*** **de gozaru**
imasu / iru *(be [located] – people, animals)*	**orimasu** **oru**	**irasshaimasu*** **irassharu**
arimasu / aru *(be [located] – plants, things)*	**gozaimasu*** **gozaru**	**gozaimasu*** **gozaru**
kimasu / kuru *(come)*	**mairimasu** **mairu**	**irasshaimasu*** **irassharu**
shimasu / suru *(do)*	**itashimasu** **itasu**	**nasaimasu*** **nasaru**
tabemasu / taberu *(eat)*	**itadakimasu** **itadaku**	**meshiagarimasu** **meshiagaru**
yarimasu / yaru *(give)*	**sashiagemasu** **sashiageru**	**kudasaimasu*** **kudasaru**
ikimasu / iku *(go)*	**mairimasu** **mairu**	**irasshaimasu*** **irassharu**
iimasu / iu *(say)*	**mōshimasu** **mōsu**	**osshaimasu*** **ossharu**
mimasu / miru *(see)*	**haiken shimasu** **haiken suru**	**goran nasaimasu*** **goran nasaru**

Note also that the Honorific **irassharu** is used for the verbs *go, come,* and *be [located]* , **mairu** is used for both *go* and *come,* and **gozaru** is used whether the subject is the speaker or someone else.

HONORIFIC VERB ENDINGS

It is possible to make any Neutral verb Exalted by either changing the verb to the Passive Form *(See Chapter 10, Base 1 Endings: -reru, -rareru)* or using the formula **o-[V2] ni naru.** Following are examples of both forms.

Ex.: **Shachō-san to hanasaremashita ka?**
  Shachō-san to o-hanashi ni narimashita ka?
  Did you speak with the company president?

  Nanigo o oshieraremasu ka?
  Nanigo o o-oshie ni narimasu ka?
  What language do you teach?

Certain of the Neutral verbs listed on the previous page are also sometimes made Exalted by one or the other (or both, in some cases) of these formulas, as follows:

Ex.: **Nanika taberaremasen ka?**
  Nanika o-tabe ni narimasen ka?
  Won't you eat something?

  Ano kata wa nan to iwaremashita ka?
  What did that person say?

  Kon'ya koraremasen ka shira.
  I wonder if you wouldn't be able to come this evening.

By the same token, a Neutral verb may be made Humble by using the formula **o-[V2] shimasu** or **o-[V2] itashimasu.** (**Itashimasu** is considered more humble than **shimasu.**)

Ex.: **Sensei no nimotsu o o-mochi shimashō.**
  I will (Let me) carry the teacher's luggage.
  Sono koto o shachō-san ni o-hanashi itashimashita.
  I spoke about that matter with the company president.

Two-word **"suru"** verbs are similarly handled:

Ex.: **Ashita o-denwa itashimasu/shimasu.** *I will telephone tomorrow.*

A polite request is made more polite by the formula **o-[V2 /Noun form] kudasai/kudasaimase.**

Ex.: **Sensei to o-hanashi kudasai.** *Please speak with the instructor.*
  Ashita o-denwa kudasaimase. *Please telephone [me] tomorrow.*

ADJECTIVES

In very formal or literary speech, special adjective forms are used:

Ex.: **Yoroshū gozaimasu.** *It's okay/good. (from Yoroshii desu.)*
  Chikō gozaimasu. *It's nearby. (from Chikai desu.)*
  Shirō gozaimasu. *It's white. (from Shiroi desu.)*

38. Numbers

Basic cardinal numbers are listed below. Note that there is more than one form for certain numbers. Both forms are common and should be learned.

0	rei/zero	*100*	hyaku
1	ichi	*1,000*	sen/issen
2	ni	*10,000*	man/ichiman
3	san	*100,000*	jū-man
4	shi/yon	*1,000,000*	hyaku-man
5	go	*10,000,000*	sen-man/issen-man
6	roku	*100,000,000*	oku/ichi-oku
7	shichi/nana	*1,000,000,000*	jū-oku
8	hachi	*10,000,000,000*	hyaku-oku
9	ku/kyū	*100,000,000,000*	sen-oku/issen-oku
10	jū	*1,000,000,000,000*	chō/itchō

11-19: jū + the remaining number

jū-ichi *(11)*, jū-ni *(12)*, jū-san *(13)*, jū-shi/jū-yon *(14)*, jū-go *(15)*, jū-roku *(16)*, jū-shichi/jū-nana *(17)*, jū-hachi *(18)*, jū-ku/jū-kyū *(19)*

Multiples of *10:* Multiplier + jū

nijū *(20)*, sanjū *(30)*, yonjū *(40)*, gojū *(50)*, rokujū *(60)*, nanajū [less common is shichijū] *(70)*, hachijū *(80)*, kyūjū *(90)*

Multiples of *100:* Multiplier + hyaku or a variant (*)

nihyaku *(200)*, sanbyaku* *(300)*, yonhyaku *(400)*, gohyaku *(500)*, roppyaku* *(600)*, nanahyaku *(700)*, happyaku* *(800)*, kyūhyaku *(900)*

Multiples of *1,000:* Multiplier + sen or a variant (*)

nisen *(2,000)*, sanzen* *(3,000)*, yonsen *(4,000)*, gosen *(5,000)*, rokusen *(6,000)*, nanasen *(7,000)*, hassen* *(8,000)*, kyūsen *(9,000)*

Multiples of *10,000:* Multiplier + man

niman *(20,000)*, sanman *(30,000)*, yonman *(40,000)*, goman *(50,000)*, rokuman *(60,000)*, nanaman [less common is shichiman] *(70,000)*, hachiman *(80,000)*, kyūman *(90,000)*

Multiples of *100,000:* Multiplier + jū-man

nijū-man *(200,000)*, sanjū-man *(300,000)*, yonjū-man *(400,000)*, gojū-man *(500,000)*, rokujū-man *(600,000)*, nanajū-man *(700,000)*, hachijū-man *(800,000)*, kyūjū-man *(900,000)*

Multiples of *1,000,000:* Multiplier + hyaku-man or a variant (*)

nihyaku-man *(2,000,000)*, sanbyaku-man* *(3,000,000)*, yonhyaku-man *(4,000,000)*, gohyaku-man *(5,000,000)*, roppyaku-man* *(6,000,000)*, nanahyaku-man *(7,000,000)*, happyaku-man* *(8,000,000)*, kyūhyaku-man *(9,000,000)*

<u>Multiples of *10,000,000:*</u> Multiplier + sen-man or a variant (*)
nisen-man *(20,000,000),* sanzen-man* *(30,000,000),* yonsen-man
(40,000,000), gosen-man *(50,000,000),* rokusen-man *(60,000,000),*
nanasen-man *(70,000,000),* hassen-man* *(80,000,000),* kyūsen-man
(90,000,000)

Multiples of **oku** and **chō** follow the above patterns. The creation of large
numbers requires no particle: *1,234,567,891,234* = **itchō, nisen-sanbyaku-
yonjūgo-oku, rokusen-nanahyaku-hachijūkyū-man,** [is]**sen-nihyaku-sanjū-yon.**

MATH

bunsū	*(fraction)*	**hiku**	*(to subtract)*
1/2	**nibun no ichi / hanbun**	**kazu, sū**	*number, digit*
1/3	**sanbun no ichi**	**keisan suru**	*(to calculate)*
1/4	**yonbun no ichi**	**sansū**	*(arithmetic)*
2/3	**sanbun no ni**	**sūgaku**	*(mathematics)*
3/4	**yonbun no san**	**tashizan**	*(addition)*
1/10	**jūbun no ichi**	**tasu**	*(to add)*
hikizan	*(subtraction)*	**ten**	*([decimal] point)*

Ex.: **Jū kara ni o hiku to, hachi ni narimasu.**
Jū hiku ni wa hachi desu.
Ten minus two equals eight.
Gojū-san ni yonjū-nana o tasu to, hyaku ni narimasu.
Gojū-san tasu yonjū-nana wa hyaku desu.
Fifty-three plus forty-seven equals one hundred.
Taion wa kashi kyūjūhachi-ten-roku-do desu.
Your body temperature is 98.6 degrees Fahrenheit.

MONEY

en *(yen—Japanese monetary unit)*   **doru** *(dollar)*
                                          sento *(cent)*

Ex.: **Goman-en de kaimashita.** *I bought it for 50,000 yen.*
Amerika no okane wa jū-doru shika motte imasen.
I don't have but $10 of American money.
Nedan wa nijūgo-doru, kyūjū-kyū-sento desu. *The price is $25.99.*

ORDINAL NUMBERS

To express "number [one, two, etc.]," add the suffix **-ban** after the
number: **ichiban, niban, sanban,** and so on.

To express "first," "second," "third," add **-banme: ichibanme, nibanme,
sanbanme,** etc.

39. Counters

The Japanese system of counting items includes a catalog of suffixes called "counters" or "classifiers," that are used to count particular kinds of items, dates, age, people, and so on.

Some of these counters are attached to the Chinese-derived number system presented in the previous chapter (**ichi, ni, san,** etc.); others are used with native Japanese numbers, of which only the first ten are used.

The native Japanese numbers one through ten are as follows:

1	**hito**	*6*	**mu**
2	**futa**	*7*	**nana**
3	**mi**	*8*	**ya**
4	**yo**	*9*	**kokono**
5	**itsu**	*10*	**tō**

There are two major sentence patterns for telling how many of something there are, as follows:

A. (Item) **wa** (counter) **arimasu.**

B. (Counter) **no** (item) **ga arimasu.**

Pattern A seems to be preferred for ordinary conversation; pattern B is often used in a response situation. Note that the counter in pattern A is not followed by a particle, but acts as an adverb, modifying the verb **arimasu.**

Ex.: **Tokei wa itsutsu arimasu.**
  Itsutsu no tokei ga arimasu.
  I have (There are) five watches.

The chart on the next two pages includes the counters most commonly used in daily conversation in Japan. You should be aware that there are many different counters in use; only the most common and useful are included here.

The "general counter" (**hitotsu, futatsu, mittsu,** etc.) can be used in place of many other counters when the specific counter is not known. It should not, however, be used in place of the counter for people.

Counters for hours of the day, days of the month, years, etc., are presented in Chapter 41, *Specific Time.*

Usage

Question	One	Two	Three	Four	Five
Six	Seven	Eight	Nine	Ten	Over Ten
General Counter (miscellaneous)					
ikutsu	hitotsu	futatsu	mittsu	yottsu	itsutsu
muttsu	nanatsu	yattsu	kokonotsu	tō	(# only)
People					
nannin	hitori	futari	sannin	yonin	gonin
rokunin	nananin, shichinin	hachinin	kyūnin	jūnin	(# + nin)
Years of Age					
nansai	issai	nisai	sansai	yonsai	gosai
rokusai	nanasai	hassai	kyūsai	jussai	(# + sai)
(Exception: *20 yrs. old* = hatachi)					
Large Animals (horses, cows, etc.)					
nantō	ittō	nitō	santō	yontō	gotō
rokutō	nanatō	hattō, hachitō	kyūtō	juttō	(# + tō)
Small Animals (cats, dogs, etc.)					
nanbiki	ippiki	nihiki	sanbiki	yonhiki	gohiki
roppiki	nanahiki, shichihiki	happiki	kyūhiki	juppiki	(# + hiki)
Flying & Hopping Animals (birds, frogs, etc.)					
nanba	ichiwa	niwa	sanba	yonwa	gowa
rokuwa, roppa	nanawa, shichiwa	hachiwa, happa	kyūwa	jūwa, juppa	(# + wa)
Vehicles					
nandai	ichidai	nidai	sandai	yondai	godai
rokudai	nanadai, shichidai	hachidai	kyūdai	jūdai	(# + dai)
Long, Slender Objects (pens, fingers, trees, etc.)					
nanbon	ippon	nihon	sanbon	yonhon	gohon
roppon, rokuhon	nanahon	happon	kyūhon	juppon	(# + hon)
Flat Objects (paper, stamps, shirts, etc.)					
nanmai	ichimai	nimai	sanmai	yonmai	gomai
rokumai	nanamai, shichimai	hachimai	kyūmai	jūmai	(# + mai)
Small, Non-descript Objects					
nanko	ikko	niko	sanko	yonko	goko
rokko	nanako	hachiko	kyūko	jukko	(# + ko)
Books, Volumes					
nansatsu	issatsu	nisatsu	sansatsu	yonsatsu	gosatsu
rokusatsu	nanasatsu	hassatsu	kyūsatsu	jussatsu	(# + satsu)
Cupfuls					
nanbai	ippai	nihai	sanbai	yonhai	gohai
rokuhai, roppai	nanahai	hachihai, happai	kyūhai	juppai	(# + hai)
Slices					
ikukire	hitokire	futakire	mikire	yokire	itsukire
mukire	nanakire	yakire	kyūkire	jukkire	(# + kire)
Servings of Food					
nanninmae	ichininmae	nininmae	sanninmae	yoninmae	goninmae
rokuninmae	nananinmae, shichininmae	hachininmae	kyūninmae	jūninmae	(# + ninmae)
Suits of Clothing					
nanchaku	itchaku	nichaku	sanchaku	yonchaku	gochaku
rokuchaku	nanachaku	hatchaku	kyūchaku	jutchaku	(# + chaku)

(Chart continues on next page.)

(Continued from previous page.)

Usage					
Question	One	Two	Three	Four	Five
Six	Seven	Eight	Nine	Ten	Over Ten
Pairs of Footwear					
nansoku	issoku	nisoku	sansoku	yonsoku	gosoku
rokusoku	nanasoku	hassoku	kyūsoku	jussoku	(# + soku)
"Times," Rounds					
nankai	ikkai	nikai	sankai	yonkai	gokai
rokkai	nanakai	hachikai	kyūkai	jukkai	(# + kai)
"Times," Degrees					
nando	ichido	nido	sando	yondo	godo
rokudo	shichido	hachido	kyūdo	jūdo	(# + do)
Lessons					
nanka	ikka	nika	sanka	yonka	goka
rokka	nanaka	hakka	kyūka	jukka	(# + ka)
Houses, Buildings					
nangen, nanken	ikken	niken	sangen	yonken	goken
rokken	nanaken	hachiken, hakken	kyūken	jukken	(# + ken)
Tatami Mats					
nanjō	ichijō	nijō	sanjō	yonjō	gojō
rokujō	nanajō, shichijō	hachijō	kyūjō	jūjō	(# + jō)
Floors of a Building					
nangai, nankai	ikkai	nikai	sangai	yonkai	gokai
rokkai	nanakai	hakkai, hachikai	kyūkai	jukkai	(# + kai)

COMMON EXPRESSIONS WITH COUNTERS

The following expressions are used not only with counters, but with other expressions of quantity, such as **sukoshi** and **sū[jitsu]**.

[Ctr +] zutsu   *apiece, each*
>   Ex.:   **Ringo wa hitotsu zutso kodomo ni yarimashita.**
>   *We gave one apple to each child.*

[Ctr +] oki ni   *every other*
>   Ex.:   **Ikkagetsu oki ni kai ga hirakaremasu.**
>   *Meetings are held every other month.*

[Ctr +] goto ni   *every, at intervals of*
>   Ex.:   **Kusuri wa yojikan goto ni nomu no desu.**
>   *You take the medicine every four hours.*
>   **Nika goto ni shiken ga arimasu.**
>   *We have an exam every two lessons.*

[Ctr +] buri   *after [a period of time]*
>   Ex.:   **Gonen buri [de/ni] tomodachi ni aimashita.**
>   *I met my friend after a lapse of five years.*

40. Relative Time

"Relative Time" refers to time expressions that depend on when "now" is: *today, tomorrow, last week, next year, every morning,* etc. Time expressions usually come either immediately before or just after the topic.

saki/mae (before, previously)		ima (now)	ato [de] (later, afterwards)	
mukashi (long ago, anciently)		saikin (recently)	shōrai ([in the] future)	
ototoi (day before yesterday)	kinō (yesterday)	kyō (today)	ashita, asu (tomorrow)	asatte (day after tomorrow)
ototoi no asa (morning before last)	kinō no asa (yesterday morning)	kesa (this morning)	ashita no asa (tomorrow morning)	asatte no asa (morning after tomorrow)
ototoi no ban (night before last)	sakuban, yūbe (last night)	konban (tonight)	ashita no ban, ashita no yoru (tomorrow night)	asatte no ban, asatte no yoru (night after tomorrow)
sen-senshū (week before last)	senshū (last week)	konshū (this week)	raishū (next week)	saraishū (week after next)
sen-sengetsu (month before last)	sengetsu (last month)	kongetsu (this month)	raigetsu (next month)	saraigetsu (month after next)
ototoshi (year before last)	kyonen (last year)	kotoshi (this year)	rainen (next year)	sarainen (year after next)

maiasa (every morning)	mainichi (every day)
maiban (every evening)	maishū (every week)
mainen, maitoshi (every year)	maitsuki (every month)

itsumo (always)	mazu (first [of all])
kesshite (never)	mō (already)
kono goro (about this time, lately)	[mō] sugu (soon, right away)
kore kara (hereafter)	sore kara (after that, then)
mada ([not] yet, still)	

The particle **ni**, which is used to mark Specific Time expressions *(See Chapter 41),* is not needed after Relative Time expressions.

Ex.: **Ashita doko ni ikimasu ka?** *Where are you going tomorrow?*
Tanaka-san wa senshū Hawai ni imashita.
Tanaka was in Hawaii last week.

Wa is used when the Relative Time word is the subject of the sentence; other particles are used whenever appropriate.

Ex.: **Kyō wa Doyōbi desu.** *Today is Saturday.*
Ashita made matte kudasai. *Please wait until tomorrow.*

41. Specific Time

"Specific Time" expressions refer to points in time that do not change according to when "now" is—hours of the clock, days of the week/month, months of the year, etc. In other words, Monday is always Monday, even if today is Tuesday; 2:00 is always 2:00, no matter what time it is now; 1999 is always that year, no matter what this year is; and so on.

TIME OF DAY

The suffix **-ji** indicates hours of the clock; **-fun/-pun** indicates minutes. When telling the time, the hour is given first, then the minutes, as in English: **sanji-juppun** *(3:10)*. Corresponding interrogatives are **nanji** *(what time?/what hour of the clock?)* and **nanpun** *(how many minutes [past the hour]?)*

1:00	ichiji	*:01*	ippun	*:13*	jūsanpun	*:25*	nijūgofun
2:00	niji	*:02*	nifun	*:14*	jūyonpun	*:26*	nijūroppun,
3:00	sanji	*:03*	sanpun	*:15*	jūgofun		nijūrokufun
4:00	yoji*	*:04*	yonpun	*:16*	jūroppun,	*:27*	nijūnanafun
5:00	goji	*:05*	gofun		jūrokufun	*:28*	nijūhappun,
6:00	rokuji	*:06*	roppun,	*:17*	jūnanafun		nijūhachifun
7:00	shichiji		rokufun	*:18*	jūhappun,	*:29*	nijūkyūfun
8:00	hachiji	*:07*	nanafun		jūhachifun	*:30*	sanjuppun**
9:00	kuji	*:08*	happun,	*:19*	jūkyūfun	*:31*	sanjūippun
10:00	jūji		hachifun	*:20*	nijuppun	*:32*	sanjūnifun
11:00	jūichiji	*:09*	kyūfun	*:21*	nijūippun	*:33*	sanjūsanpun
12:00	jūniji	*:10*	juppun	*:22*	nijūnifun	*:34*	sanjūyonpun
(The 24-hour clock		*:11*	jūippun	*:23*	nijūsanpun	(and so on, in
continues in the		*:12*	jūnifun	*:24*	nijūyonpun	pattern, through
same pattern.)						*:60*	rokujuppun)

*Note that 4:00 is **yoji**, rather than *yonji*.
The half hour can also be expressed by adding -han to the hour: **ichiji-han *(1:30)*.

The expressions **gogo** *(p.m.)*, **gozen** *(a.m.)*, and **chōdo** *(exactly)* always *precede* the time.

Ex.: **gogo rokuji** *(6:00 p.m.)*
gozen hachiji-han *(8:30 a.m.)*
chōdo jūji *(exactly 10:00)*
chōdo gozen shichiji *(exactly 7:00 a.m.)*

The expressions **goro** *(approximately)*, **mae** *(before)*, and **sugi** *(after)*, *follow* the time.

Ex.: **yoji goro** *(approximately 4:00)*, **gogo sanji goro** *(about 3:00 p.m.)*
niji juppun mae *(ten minutes before two)*
rokuji jūgofun sugi *(15 minutes after 6)*

DAYS OF THE WEEK & MONTH

Nichiyōbi *(Sunday)*   Mokuyōbi *(Thursday)*
Getsuyōbi *(Monday)*   Kin'yōbi *(Friday)*
Kayōbi *(Tuesday)*   Doyōbi *(Saturday)*
Suiyōbi *(Wednesday)*   nan'yōbi/naniyōbi *(what day of the week?)*

Days of the Month:

1	tsuitachi	*11*	jūichi-nichi	*21*	nijūichi-nichi
2	futsuka	*12*	jūni-nichi	*22*	nijūni-nichi
3	mikka	*13*	jūsan-nichi	*23*	nijūsan-nichi
4	yokka	*14*	jūyokka	*24*	nijūyokka
5	itsuka	*15*	jūgo-nichi	*25*	nijūgo-nichi
6	muika	*16*	jūroku-nichi	*26*	nijūroku-nichi
7	nanoka	*17*	jūshichi-nichi	*27*	nijūshichi-nichi
8	yōka	*18*	jūhachi-nichi	*28*	nijūhachi-nichi
9	kokonoka	*19*	jūku-nichi	*29*	nijūku-nichi
10	tōka	*20*	hatsuka	*30*	sanjū-nichi

nannichi = *what day of the month? what date?*   *31* sanjūichi-nichi

MONTHS OF THE YEAR

Ichigatsu *(January)*   Gogatsu *(May)*   Kugatsu *(September)*
Nigatsu *(February)*   Rokugatsu *(June)*   Jūgatsu *(October)*
Sangatsu *(March)*   Shichigatsu *(July)*   Jūichigatsu *(November)*
Shigatsu *(April)*   Hachigatsu *(August)*   Jūnigatsu *(December)*
nangatsu = *what month?*

YEARS: WESTERN CALENDAR

The suffix **-nen** follows the number of the year in the Western calendar: **sen-kyūhyaku-kyūjū-kyū-nen** *(1999)*. The corresponding interrogative is **nannen** *(what year?)*.

Ex.:   **Nannen ni umaremashita ka?** *[In] what year were you born?*
Kotoshi wa nannen desu ka? *What year is this [year]?*
Sen-kyūhyaku-nijū-san-nen ni Kantō chihō de daijishin ga okorimashita.
In 1923 a great earthquake occurred in the Kanto district.

The words **kigen** *(A.D.)* and **kigenzen** *(B.C.)* precede the Western calendar year:

Ex.:   **Kigen yonhyaku-nijū-ichi-nen** *(421 A.D.)*
Kigenzen roppyaku-nen goro *(about 600 B.C.)*

YEARS: JAPANESE IMPERIAL CALENDAR

Traditionally the Japanese have counted years according to the reigning emperor or the family or individual in power. Currently an Imperial Era begins when an emperor dies and his heir ascends the throne. The new emperor chooses a name by which both he and the incoming era will be known.

The current era is called **Heisei** *(accomplishment of peace/peaceful accomplishment)*, the name chosen by Emperor Akihito after his father Hirohito's death on January 7, 1989, and the Heisei Era began on that date. The first year of any Imperial Era is called **gannen** *(original year)*; therefore, 1989 is **Heisei gannen** by the Japanese calendar. 1990 is **Heisei ninen**, 1991 is **Heisei sannen**, and so on. Names of the previous three eras are:

Shōwa *(1926-1988)*   Taishō *(1912-1926)*   Meiji *(1868-1912)*

To convert a Western Calendar year to Imperial Calendar time, subtract the number of the year prior to the first year of the concurrent Imperial era from the Western Calendar year. Reverse the process to convert Imperial years to Western years.

Ex.: 1997 (-1988) = **Heisei 9-nen**   Taishō **12-nen** (+ 1911) = 1923
      1945 (-1925) = **Shōwa 20-nen**   Meiji **6-nen** (+ 1867) = 1873

USING SPECIFIC TIME IN A SENTENCE

The order of a date is from largest increment to smallest.

Ex.: **1935-nen, Nigatsu, jūyokka, Mokuyōbi** *(Thursday, February 14, 1935)*

The usual particle for Specific Time is **ni**. When an activity begins or ends at a certain time, **kara** or **made** may be used.

Ex.: **Mainichi nanji ni okimasu ka?** *What time do you get up every day?*
      Gozen jūji-han ni tsukimashita. *I arrived at 10:30 A.M.*
      Ima nanji nanpun desu ka? *What time is it now [exactly]?*
      Chōdo rokuji kara hajimarimasu. *We will begin at exactly 6:00.*
      Ichiji kara goji made hatarakimashita. *I worked from 1:00 to 5:00.*

TIME DURATION

Use the suffix **-kan** for periods of hours, minutes, or years; use **-shūkan** for so many weeks, **-kagetsu** for so many months.

ichijikan *(1 hour)*	ippunkan *(1 minute)*	ichinenkan *(1 year)*
nijikan *(2 hours)*	nifunkan *(2 minutes)*	ninenkan *(2 years)*
sanjikan *(3 hours)*	sanpunkan *(3 minutes)*	sannenkan *(3 years)*
yojikan *(4 hours)*	yonpunkan *(4 minutes)*	yonenkan *(4 years)*
nanjikan *(how many hrs?)*	nanpunkan *(. . . mins?)*	nannenkan *(. . . yrs?)*

isshūkan *(1 week)*	ikkagetsu *(1 month)*
nishūkan *(2 weeks)*	nikagetsu *(2 months)*
sanshūkan *(3 weeks)*	sankagetsu *(3 months)*
yonshūkan *(4 weeks)*	yonkagetsu *(4 months)*
nanshūkan *(how many wks?)*	nankagetsu *(how many months?)*

Except for **tsuitachi**, the words for days of the month are also used for a period of days; ie, **mikka** *(third day of the month)* can also mean "three days' time." A period of one day is **ichinichi**. Interrogative: **nannichi-kan** or **nannichi gurai** *(about how many days?)*.

42. Seasons & the Weather

The Four Seasons: **haru** *(spring)*   **aki** *(autumn)*
                   natsu *(summer)*   **fuyu** *(winter)*

It is common for the Japanese to make a comment about the weather to open a conversation or a letter, even a business letter. Following are some useful expressions and sentence patterns for commenting on the weather.

ame *(rain)*
arashi *(storm)*
atatakai *(warm)*
atsui *(hot)*
aozora *(blue sky)*
-do *(degrees [of temperature])*
fuku *(to blow [wind])*
furu *(to fall [rain, snow])*
hare *(a clear day)*
hareru *(to clear up)*
inazuma *(lightning)*
kaminari *(thunder)*
kaze *(wind)*
kion *(temperature)*
kiri *(fog)*
kisetsu *(season)*

kumo *(cloud)*
kumori *(a cloudy day)*
kumoru *(to cloud up)*
mushiatsui *(hot & humid, sultry)*
niji *(rainbow)*
ōame *(heavy rain)*
ondokei *(thermometer)*
samui *(cold [weather])*
shiki *(four seasons)*
sora *(sky)*
suzushii *(cool)*
taifū *(typhoon)*
[o-]tenki *(weather)*
tenki yohō *(weather report)*
tsuyu *(rainy season)*
yuki *(snow)*

Ex.: **Ii o-tenki desu, ne!** *It's a nice day, isn't it? (Lit. It's good weather . . .)*
Yuki ga futte imasu. *It's snowing. (Lit. The snow is falling.)*
Kaze ga fuite imasu. *The wind is blowing.*
Kinō ame deshita ga, kyō wa harete imasu.
  Yesterday it was rain[y], but today it has cleared up.
Kyō kumotte iru kara suzushii desu. *It's cool today because it's cloudy.*
Saikin ame ga yoku furimasu, ne. *It rains a lot lately, doesn't it?*
Tenki yohō wa dō desu ka? *How is the weather forecast?*
Ondokei wa sesshi nijū-do desu.
  The thermometer says (is) 20 degrees Centigrade.

TEMPERATURE COMPARISON

Sesshi *(Centigrade)*	Kashi *(Fahrenheit)*
0°	32°
10°	50°
20°	68°
30°	86°
37°	98.6°
40°	104°
100°	212°

43. The Family

Different words are used by the Japanese for "my" family and "your" family. Words for "your" family are more polite and can refer to the person being addressed or some other person to show respect. In the following list, where there are two words for "my" family, the first is a neutral word that can also be used to refer to mothers, fathers, etc., in general.

My Family		Your Family
haha, okāsan	*mother*	okāsan
chichi, otōsan	*father*	otōsan
ani, oniisan	*older brother*	oniisan
ane, onēsan	*older sister*	onēsan
otōto	*younger brother*	otōto-san
imōto	*younger sister*	imōto-san
musuko	*son*	musuko-san
musume	*daughter*	musume-san, ojō-san
kazoku	*family*	go-kazoku
kodomo, ko	*child*	o-ko-san
oya, ryōshin	*parents*	go-ryōshin
oji, ojisan	*uncle*	ojisan
oba, obasan	*aunt*	obasan
sofu, ojiisan	*grandfather*	ojiisan
sobo, obāsan	*grandmother*	obāsan
tsuma, kanai	*wife*	okusan, okusama
shujin	*husband*	go-shujin

OTHER HOME/FAMILY-RELATED WORDS

dokushin *(single [person])*
fūfu *(married couple)*
fujin *(lady, woman, Mrs.)*
giri no [haha] *([mother]-in-law)*
itoko *(cousin)*
katei *(home)*
kekkon suru *(to get married)*
kyōdai *(brothers [& sisters], siblings)*
mago *(grandchild)*

mei *(niece)*
muko *(son-in-law)*
oi *(nephew)*
oyako *(parent and child)*
senzo *(ancestors)*
shimai *(sisters)*
shinseki *(relatives)*
yome *(daughter-in-law)*

Ex.: **Go-kazoku wa nannin desu ka?** *How many people are in your family?*
Yonin desu. Ani ga futari to imōto ga hitori desu. *

> *There are (It is) four people. I have (There are) two older brothers and one younger sister.*

*"Yonin" here refers to four children in the family. The Japanese assume that there are parents, and so they are not included in the count.

44. Health & the Body

BODY PARTS

ago *(chin)*
ashi *(leg, foot)*
ashikubi *(ankle)*
atama *(head)*
ha *(tooth)*
hana *(nose)*
hara, onaka *(stomach)*
heso *(navel)*
hiji *(elbow)*
hitai, odeko *(forehead)*
hiza *(knee)*
hō, hoho *(cheek)*
kami [no ke] *(hair)*
kao *(face)*
karada *(body)*
kata *(shoulder)*

koshi *(waist, hips)*
kubi *(neck)*
kuchi *(mouth)*
kuchibiru *(lips)*
me *(eye)*
mimi *(ear)*
mune *(chest, breast)*
nodo *(throat)*
[o-] shiri *(hips, posterior)*
senaka *(back)*
shita *(tongue)*
te *(hand)*
tekubi *(wrist)*
ude *(arm)*
yubi *(finger, toe)*

OTHER HEALTH VOCABULARY

arerugii *(allergy)*
asupirin *(aspirin)*
bandoeido *(band-aid)*
bitamin *(vitamin)*
byōin *(hospital)*
byōki *(sick; illness)*
genki *(healthy)*
geri *(diarrhea)*
geri-dome *(diarrhea medicine)*
haisha *(dentist)*
i-no-mukatsuki *(nausea)*
isha *(doctor)*
itai [desu] *([It is] painful)*
kaze [o hiku] *([to catch] a cold)*
kayui *(itchy)*
kazegusuri *(cold medicine)*

kega o suru *(to be injured)*
kizu *(wound, injury)*
kizugusuri *(ointment for wounds)*
kizutsukeru *(to wound, injure)*
kushami [o suru] *(sneeze [to sneeze])*
kusuri *(medicine)*
mizumushi *(athlete's foot)*
mushiba *(decayed tooth)*
netsu [ga aru] *([have a] fever)*
nomisugi *(overdrinking)*
seki [o suru] *(cough [to cough])*
shohō[sen] *(prescription)*
shōkafuryō *(indigestion)*
tabesugi *(overeating)*
torōchi *(throat lozenge)*
zutsū [ga aru/suru] *([have a] headache)*

Ex.: **Doko ga itai desu ka?** *Where does it hurt?*
Senaka ga itai desu. *My back hurts.*
Koko ga itai desu. *It hurts here.*
Chotto byōki desu. *I am a little bit sick.*
O-isha-san ni denwa o shite kudasai. *Please call the doctor.*
Netsu ga arimasu ga, asupirin wa arimasen ka?
I have a fever; don't you have some aspirin?

45. Wearing Clothes

In Japanese there are several verbs meaning "to wear," depending on the type of clothing or accessories referred to.

haku *(for things worn on the lower part of the body: shoes, socks, pants, skirt)*

kaburu *(hats, headgear—Lit. to put over the head)*

kakeru *(glasses—Lit. to hang)*

kiru *(clothes worn on the upper torso; also for clothes in general)*

maku *(for scarves, mufflers—Lit. to wrap)*

tsukeru *(for jewelry, flowers, adornments —Lit. to attach)*

shimeru *(for neckties, sashes, belts—Lit. to fasten, tie)*

suru *(for small pieces of clothing or jewelry—Lit. to do)*

Ex.: **Kutsu o haite dekakemashita.** *He put on his shoes and went out.*

Burū no sukāto o hakō to omoimasu.
I think I will wear the blue skirt.

Bōshi o kabutte iru hito wa dare desu ka?
Who is the person wearing the hat?

Megane o kakenai to miru koto ga dekimasen.
I can't see if I don't wear glasses.

Atsui node, uwagi o kinaide ikimasu.
Because it's hot, I will go without [wearing] a coat.

Kimono o kiru ka yōfuku o kiru ka, hayaku kimenai to dame desu.
You have to decide quickly whether you are going to wear a kimono or Western clothing.

Tsuyoi kaze ga fuite iru kara, erimaki o maite ikimasu.
A strong wind is blowing, so I will wear a neck scarf [and go].

Ano hito wa itsumo hana o kami ni tsukemasu.
That person always wears a flower in her hair.

Kono burōchi o tsukete mo ii to omoimasu ka?
Do you think it's okay to wear this brooch?

Suzuki-san wa akai nekutai o shimete imashita.
Suzuki was wearing a red necktie.

Obi o shimesugite kurushii desu.
I tied my sashes too tight, and it's painful.

Hōseki o suru no wa kirai desu. *I hate wearing jewelry.*

Otōsan wa itsumo nekutai o shimasu, ne?
Your father always wears a necktie, doesn't he?

Nugu *(take off, remove)* is used for any type of clothing.

Ex.: **Kutsu o nuide haitte kudasai.** *Please take off your shoes and enter.*

Atsui kara uwagi o nuide okimashō.
Since it's hot, let's take off our suitcoats.

Kimono o nuide kara, kono yukata o kite mo ii desu.
After taking off the kimono, you may wear this summer kimono.

46. Common Expressions & Useful Vocabulary

HELLOS, GOODBYES, & INTRODUCTIONS

Ohayō gozaimasu. *Good morning.*
Konnichi wa. *Hello. (daytime)*
Konban wa. *Good evening.*
Sayōnara. *Goodbye.*
O-yasumi nasai. *Good night.*
Dewa mata. / Jā mata. *See you later. / So long.*
O-genki desu ka? *How are you? (Lit. Are you healthy?)*
O-kage-sama de, genki desu. *I'm fine, thank you.*
O-genki de. *Take care. (Lit. Be healthy.)*
O-namae wa nan desu ka? *What is your name?*
[My name] to mōshimasu. *I am called/My name is _____.*
Hajimemashite. *I'm happy to meet you.*
[Dōzo] yoroshiku [o-negai shimasu]. *Please accept my regards.*
Itte kimasu/mairimasu. *I'll be back.*
Itte irasshai. *See you. (Lit. Go and come [back].)*
Tadaima. *I'm back./I'm home. (Lit. Just now.)*
O-kaerinasai. *Welcome back.*

THANK-YOU'S & APOLOGIES

[Dōmo] arigatō gozaimasu. *Thank you [very much].*
Dō itashimashite. *You're welcome./It's nothing.*
Kochira koso. *The pleasure is mine.*
Go-enryo naku. *Go ahead./Don't hesitate.*
Go-yukkuri. *Take your time.*
Go-kurōsama deshita. *Thank you for your efforts.*
O-machidōsama deshita. *Thank you for waiting.*
Sumimasen. *Excuse me. / Thank you.*
Gomen nasai. *I'm sorry. / Forgive me.*
Mōshiwake gozaimasen. *I have no excuse. (I'm very sorry.)*
O-wabi itashimasu. *I apologize.*
Zannen desu. *That's too bad.*
[O-]ki no doku desu. *I'm sorry to hear it. (Lit. It is poison to the spirit.)*
Shitsurei shimasu. *Excuse me for my rudeness.*
O-jama shimasu. *Excuse me for bothering you.*
O-saki ni shitsurei shimasu. *Excuse me for going ahead of you.*
O-saki ni dōzo. *Please go ahead of me.*

DINING OUT

O-naka ga suite imasu/sukimashita. *I'm hungry.*
[Ocha] demo nomimasen ka? *Won't you have (drink) some [tea]?*
Menyū, o-negai shimasu. *Please [bring me] a menu.*
[Wain risuto], o-negai dekimasu ka? *May I have a [wine list]?*

[Kōhii] o kudasai.   *Please give me [some coffee].*
Nani ni shimasu ka?   *What will you have?*
[Chikin katsu] wa arimasu ka?   *Do you have [chicken cutlets]?*
[Chikin katsu] ga dekimasu ka?   *Can you make [chicken cutlets]?*
O-hiya ga hoshii desu.   *I want some ice water.*
[Kōri] nashi de, o-negai shimasu.   *No [ice], please.*
O-kawari, o-negai shimasu. / O-kawari kudasai.   *Please bring me another.*
Sarada-tsuki desu ka?   *Does that come with salad?*
Dezāto ga haitte imasu ka?   *Is dessert included?*
Oishii desu.   *It's delicious.*
[Kōhii] wa tsumetai desu.   *[The coffee] is cold.*
[Ocha] wa irimasen.   *I don't want (need) any [tea].*
O-kanjō, o-negai shimasu.   *The check, please.*
Go-chisōsama deshita.   *Thank you for the meal.*

SHOPPING

Gomen kudasai.   *Is anyone there? (to call a clerk)*
Irasshaimase.   *Welcome. Come in.*
Kore wa nan desu ka?   *What is this?*
Sore wa ikura desu ka?   *How much is that?*
_____ ga arimasu ka?   *Do you have _____?*
Chotto takai desu.   *It's a little expensive.*
Motto yasui mono wa arimasen ka?   *Don't you have something cheaper?*
[Nihon]-sei desu ka?   *Is it made in [Japan]?*
Hoka no iro ga arimasu ka?   *Do you have another color?*
Tsutsunde itadakemasu ka?   *Can I have it wrapped?*
[Ōkii hō] o itadakimasu.   *I will take [the bigger one].*
Zenbu de ikura desu ka?   *How much is it altogether?*
Ikura ni narimasu ka?   *How much does it come to?*
Kādo wa tsukaemasu ka?   *Can I use a charge card?*
Reshiito itadakemasu ka?   *Can I get a receipt?*

VISITING

Gomen kudasai.   *Is anyone home?*
Yoku irasshaimashita.   *Welcome.*
Dōzo o-agari kudasai.   *Please come in. (come up)*
Dōzo o-hairi kudasai.   *Please enter.*
O-jama shimasu.   *Excuse me for bothering you.*
Kochira e dōzo.   *This way, please.*
O-kake kudasai.   *Please sit down.*
[Ocha] demo nomimasen ka?   *Won't you have some [tea]?*
[Iie,] kekkō desu.   *[No,] that's okay.*
Shinpai shinaide kudasai.   *Please don't worry [about me].*
Kono hen de shitsurei shimasu.   *I'll be leaving now.*
Mata o-ai shimashō.   *Let's see each other again.*
Mata irasshai./Mata oide kudasai.   *Come again.*
Rusu desu.   *Nobody's home.*

TELEPHONING

denwa o suru/shimasu *to telephone, make a phone call*
denwa o kakeru/kakemasu *to telephone, make a phone call*
denwa ni deru *to come to the phone*
Moshi-moshi. *Hello. (when answering the phone)*
[name]-san desu ka? *Is this the _____ household?*
[name]-san wa irasshaimasu ka? *Is _____ there?*
Chotto matte kudasai. *Please wait a moment.*
Shōshō o-machi kudasai. *Please wait a moment. (formal)*
[name] wa ima orimasen. _____ *is not in now.*
Denwa o kawarimasu. *I'm giving the phone to someone else.*
Denwa bangō o oshiete kudasai. *Please give me your phone number.*

INTERJECTIONS & COMMENTARY

Aa, sō desu ka? *Oh, really?*
Abunai [yo]! *Danger! Look out!*
Ano ne. *By the way . . . / Say . . .*
Are! / Ara! *Ah! / Oh!*
Ashimoto ni ki o tsukete kudasai. *Watch your step.*
baka [na] *stupid*
Daijōbu desu. *It's/I'm all right.*
Dō iu imi desu ka? *What does it mean?*
Dō shiyō/shimashō [ka]? *What shall we do?*
Dōzo. *Please. (Go ahead.)*
Ganbatte kudasai. *Work hard. Give it all you've got.*
Hontō desu. *It's true.*
Jōdan ja nai yo! *Don't be ridiculous! (Lit. It's no joke.)*
Kawaisō desu. *Poor thing!*
Kekkō desu. *That's okay. No, thank you.*
Ki no doku desu. *I'm sorry to hear it.*
Ki o tsukete kudasai. *Take care. Be careful.*
Mada desu. *Not yet.*
Masaka! *Ridiculous!*
[Mō] jikan desu. *It's time [already].*
Nihongo de nan desu ka? *What is it in Japanese?*
O-medetō gozaimasu. *Congratulations.*
    Akemashite o-medetō gozaimasu. *Happy New Year.*
    [special day] o-medetō gozaimasu. *Happy [birthday, anniversary, etc.].*
O-negai shimasu. *Please. (I ask you to do it.)*
O-wasuremono nai yō ni go-chūi kudasai. *Be careful not to forget anything.*
Shikata ga nai/arimasen. *It can't be helped.*
Shinjirarenai./Shinjiraremasen. *I can't believe it. (Lit. It's unbelievable.)*
Sō ka mo shiremasen. *That may be so.*
Sono tōri desu. *That's right.*
Tanoshimi ni shite imasu. *I'm looking forward to it.*
Yokatta desu. *Thank goodness.*
Zannen desu. *That's too bad.*

VOCABULARY LISTS   The following lists are designed not as a glossary but as a categorized study aid, listing groups of related words for a systematic way of learning basic vocabulary centered around common topics. *(See also pp. 119-122.)*

KYŌIKU   *Education*
benkyō suru *to study*
gakka *subject of study*
  bakegaku, kagaku *chemistry*
  bungaku *literature*
  chigaku *geology*
  chiri *geography*
  dōbutsugaku *zoology*
  geijutsu/bijutsu *the arts/fine arts*
  gengo *[foreign] languages*
  igaku *medicine (study of)*
  kagaku *science*
  keizaigaku *economics*
  kokugo *[Japanese] language*
  rekishi *history*
  sansū *arithmetic*
  seibutsugaku *biology*
  sūgaku *mathematics*
[ichi-]gakki *[first] term, semester*
gakkō *school*
  chūgakkō *middle school*
  daigaku *university, college*
  daigakuin *graduate school*
  juku *"cram school," after-school test preparation classes*
  kōtōgakkō (kōkō) *high school*
  shōgakkō *elementary school*
  yōchien *kindergarten*
gakui *academic degree*
gakumon *learning, study*
hyakkajiten *encyclopedia*
jibiki, jisho, jiten *dictionary*
  eiwa [jiten] *English-Japanese [dictionary]*
  waei [jiten] *Japanese-English [dictionary]*
jugyō *class, lesson*
keisanki *calculator*
kenkyū suru *to research*
kōchō sensei *principal*
kōgi *lecture*
kokuban *blackboard*
kumi, kurasu *class*
kyōiku mama *mother who pressures her children to achieve academically*
kyōkasho *textbook*
kyōshitsu *classroom*
nyūgaku suru *to enter school*
rōnin *student not yet accepted into a college*
[gakusei]ryō *[student] dormitory*

seito *student*
  daigakusei *student (of a university)*
  dōkyūsei *classmate*
  gakusei *student (of a school)*
  jōkyūsei *senior student*
  kakyūsei *junior student*
  [ichi]-nensei *[first]-grader, [first]-year student,*
sensei, kyōju, kyōshi *teacher, professor, instructor*
shiken, tesuto *exam, test*
shukudai *homework*
soroban *abacus*
sotsugyō suru *to graduate*

JŪTAKU   *The Home*
daidokoro *kitchen*
engawa *veranda*
(o-)furo *bath, bathtub*
fusuma *opaque sliding door*
futon *bedding (pallet & comforter)*
genkan *entryway*
heya *room*
ie, uchi *house, home*
ima *living room*
jūsho *address*
kabe *wall*
kagu *furniture*
katei *household, home*
mado *window*
niwa *yard, garden*
ōsetsuma *drawing room, reception room*
oshiire *cupboard with sliding door*
sentaku o suru *do the laundry*
shinshitsu *bedroom*
shōji *paper sliding door/screen*
shosai *den, study*
sōji [o] suru *do the cleaning/housework*
sudare *bamboo screen*
(o-)taku *your home, you (formal)*
tatami *rice-straw mat flooring*
(o-)tearai, toire *restroom, lavatory*
tenjō *ceiling, roof*
to, doa *door*
tokonoma *alcove*
washitsu, nihonma *Japanese-style room*
yane *roof*
yōshitsu *Western-style room*
yuka *floor*

FUKU *Clothing*

wafuku *Japanese-style clothing*
  geta *wooden clogs*
  happi *hip-length kimono jacket*
  kimono *kimono*
  obi *sash for **kimono***
  tabi *socks worn w/zōri, geta*
  yukata *summer kimono*
  zōri *(straw) sandals*
yōfuku *Western-style clothing*
  beruto *belt*
  bōshi *hat, cap*
  burausu *blouse*
  doresu *dress*
  hōseki *jewelry*
  jaketto *jacket*
  kutsu *shoes*
  kutsushita *socks*
  nekutai *necktie*
  pantsu *underpants*
  shatsu *shirt*
  shitagi *underwear*
  shōtsu *shorts*
  sukāto *skirt*
  sutokkingu *stockings*
  sūtsu, sebiro *suit*
  tebukuro *gloves*
  udedokei *wristwatch*
  waishatsu *white shirt*
  zubon *pants, slacks*

TABEMONO, NOMIMONO
Food, Drink

chōmi(ryō), yakumi *seasonings, spices*
  goma *sesame seeds*
  hachimitsu *honey*
  karashi *mustard*
  koshō *pepper*
  miso *bean paste*
  satō *sugar*
  shio *salt*
  shōyu *soy sauce*
  su *vinegar*
  wasabi *horseradish sauce*
dezāto *dessert*
  aisukuriimu *ice cream*
  ame, kyandē *candy*
  bisuketto, kukkii *cracker, cookie*
  chokorēto *chocolate*
  (o-)kashi *sweets, confections*
  manjū, anpan *bean jam bun*
  mochi *sweet rice cakes*
  purin *pudding*
kokumotsu, mame *grains/cereal, beans*
  an *sweet red beans (cooked)*

  daizu *soybeans*
  genmai *unhulled rice*
  gohan *cooked rice*
  hakumai *polished rice*
  ingenmame *green/string beans*
  (o-)kome *rice (uncooked)*
  mamemoyashi *bean sprouts*
  menrui *noodles*
  mugi *wheat, barley*
  pan *bread*
  rāmen *thin, yellow wheat noodles*
  senbei, arare *rice crackers*
  shokupan *sandwich bread*
  soba *buckwheat noodles*
  udon *white wheat noodles*
kudamono *fruit*
  anzu *apricot*
  biwa *loquat*
  budō *grape*
  ichigo *strawberry*
  ichijiku *fig*
  kaki *persimmon*
  mikan *Mandarin orange*
  momo *peach*
  nashi *pear-apple (Japanese pear)*
  pain, painappuru *pineapple*
  ringo *apple*
  sakuranbo *cherry*
  suika *watermelon*
  ume *plum*
  yashinomi, kokonattsu *coconut*
niku *meat*
  butaniku *pork*
  chikinkatsu *chicken cutlet*
  gyūniku *beef*
  rebā *liver*
  tamago *egg*
  tonkatsu *pork cutlet*
  toriniku, chikin *chicken*
nomimono *drink (things to drink)*
  arukōru-sei inryō *alcoholic beverages*
  biiru *beer*
  budōshu, wain *wine*
  (o-)cha *tea*
  gyūnyū *milk*
  (o-)hiya *ice water, chilled water*
  jūsu *juice, any fruity drink*
  kōhii *coffee*
  kōri *ice*
  (o-)mizu *water*
  mugicha *barley tea*
  (o-)sake *rice wine; liquor*
  soda *soda*
  uisukii *whiskey*
nyūseihin *dairy products*

batā *butter*
chiizu *cheese*
gyūnyū, miruku *milk*
kuriimu *cream*
māgarin *margarine*
yōguruto *yogurt*
ryōri *cooking, dishes*
　donburi *bowl of cooked rice*
　hanbāgā *hamburger*
　hanbāgu *Hamburg[er] steak*
　(o-)konomiyaki *vegetable and meat
　　pancake*
　misoshiru *miso soup*
　robatayaki *hearth cooking*
　sando[itchi] *sandwich*
　sarada *salad*
　sukiyaki *meat and vegetables cooked in a
　　soy-based sauce*
　(o-)sushi *rice balls*
　sutēki, bifuteki *steak, beefsteak*
　tenpura *deep-fried shrimp, vegetables*
　teppan'yaki *hot griddle cooking*
　yakitori *skewered chicken*
sakana *fish*
　ebi *shrimp*
　ika *squid*
　kai *shellfish*
　kaki *oyster*
　maguro *tuna*
　sashimi *prepared raw fish*
　tako *octopus*
　unagi *freshwater eel*
shokuhin, shokumotsu, shokuryō *food,
　foodstuff, groceries*
shokuji *a meal*
　asagohan, chōshoku *breakfast*
　bangohan, yūshoku *dinner/supper*
　(o-)bentō *box lunch*
　chūshoku, hirugohan, ranchi *lunch*
　gohan *cooked rice; a meal*
　pikunikku *picnic*
　shokuji o suru *to have a meal, to eat dinner*
　washoku *Japanese food*
　yōshoku *Western food*
yasai *vegetables*
　daikon *large white radish*
　hakusai *Chinese cabbage*
　hōrensō *spinach*
　jagaimo *potato*
　kabocha *pumpkin*
　kinoko *mushroom*
　kyūri *cucumber*
　nasu[bi] *eggplant*
　negi *onion*

ninjin *carrot*
piiman *bell pepper, pimiento*
satsumaimo *sweet potato*
shiitake *Japanese mushroom*
takenoko *bamboo shoots*
tamanegi *round onion*
tōfu *bean curd*

JINSEI *Human Life*

adana *nickname*
akachan, akanbō *baby*
dansei *man, male*
dokushin *bachelor, spinster*
fūfu *married couple*
hito *person*
ikiru *to live*
inochi, seimei *life*
jinrui *humankind*
josei *woman, female*
keizai *genealogy, lineage*
myōji *surname*
nakayoshi *good relationship*
nakunaru *to pass away*
namae *name*
ningen *human being*
onna (no hito) *woman*
otoko (no hito) *man*
otona *adult*
seinen, wakamono *young person*
seinengappi *birth date*
shakai *society*
shi *death*
shinu *to die*
sodatsu; sodateru *to grow up; to raise/bring up*
tanjōbi *birthday*
tomodachi, yūjin *friend*
toshi, nenrei *age*
toshiyori [no] *old (person)*
tsukiau *to get to know (someone)*
umu; umareru *to give birth; to be born*
wakai *young*

SHIGOTO *Occupations*

bokushi *pastor, minister (of a church)*
buchō *department head*
daihyōsha *representative*
daijin *minister (of state)*
dairinin *agent, representative*
daitōryō *president (of the U.S.)*
enjinia *engineer*
entāteinā *entertainer*
geijutsuka *artist*
haisha *dentist*
haiyū, joyū *actor, actress*

hisho *secretary*
isha *doctor*
jieigyō [no] *self-employed*
jimuin *office clerk*
kachō *section chief*
keisatsukan *policeman*
konsarutanto *consultant*
kyōshi, sensei *teacher*
(o-)mawari-san *local police (on the beat)*
ōeru *"O.L." (office lady/worker)*
sakka *author*
sarariiman *salaryman, white collar worker*
shachō *company president*
shinpu *priest, [Catholic] father*
shōbōshi *fireman*
shoki *clerk, recorder*
sōridaijin *prime minister*
sōryo *[Buddhist] priest, monk*
supōtsuman *sportsman, athlete*
ten'in *store clerk*

GORAKU *Entertainment*

bangumi *(TV) program*
bideo [rekōdā] *video [recorder]*
channeru *(TV) channel*
eiga *movie, film*
eigakan *movie theatre*
engeki *stage play*
entāteinā *entertainer*
geinin *artist; professional entertainer*
geisha *traditional Japanese female entertainer*
gekijō *live stage theatre, playhouse*
gēmu *game*
   [shōgi]-ban *[chess] board*
   go, igo *"Go" Japanese board game*
   hanafuda, karuta *Japanese card games*
   hanetsuki *Japanese badminton*
   mājan *Mah-jong*
   pachinko *Japanese style pinball*
   shōgi *Japanese chess*
   [gēmu/supōtsu] o suru *to play [a game or sport]*
   toranpu *Western playing cards*
   yūenchi *playground*
kabuki *traditional Japanese theatre*
kamishibai *picture card streetshow*
karaoke *singing to recorded music*
kasetto *audio casette*
sākasu *circus*
shii dii *CD*
shumi *hobby, personal interest*
   amimono *knitting, needlework*
   arubamu *[photo] album*
   atsumeru, shūshū suru *to collect*

dōgu *tool, utensil, implement*
egaku *to draw/paint*
engei, niwatsukuri *horticulture, gardening*
fuirumu *(photographic) film*
hanabi *fireworks*
jū, teppō *gun, rifle*
kamera *camera*
kari, shuryō *hunting*
(o-)mocha *toy*
ongaku *music*
origami *Japanese paper folding art*
shashin [o toru] *[to take a] photograph*
shugei *handicraft*
shūshū *collecting, collection*
shūshūhin *collectibles*
sumie *black & white painting*
taiiku *physical training/education*
takoage *kite flying*
tsuri *fishing*
tsuridōgu *fishing tackle*
undō *exercise*
supōtsu *sports*
   asobu *to play* (intransitive verb)
   barēbōru *volleyball*
   basukettobōru *basketball*
   bēsubōru, yakyū *baseball*
   bokushingu *boxing*
   bōringu *bowling*
   budō, bujutsu *martial arts*
   dojjibōru *dodgeball*
   futtobōru *(American) football*
   gurando, guraundo *playing field, (sports) ground*
   hokkē *hockey*
   jidōsharēsu *car racing*
   keiba *horse racing*
   keirin *bicycle racing*
   ōtorēsu *motorcycle racing*
   puro *professional (athlete)*
   puroresu *professional wrestling*
   ragubii *rugby*
   sakkā *soccer*
   suiei *swimming*
   sukēto *skating*
   sukii *skiing*
   sumō *sumo wrestling*
   taisō *gymnastics*
sutereo *stereo*

TOKAI *The City*

bijutsukan *museum*
biru, tatemono *building*
biyōin *beauty salon*
bunbōguya *stationery store*

byōin *hospital*
chūshajō *parking lot*
depāto *department store*
eigakan *movie theater*
gekijō *drama theater*
ginkō *bank*
gofukuya *kimono store*
gyūnyūten *milk/dairy store*
hanaya *flower shop*
hon'ya *book store*
hoteru *hotel*
ichiba *market*
jinja *Shinto shrine*
kaisha *company*
kanamonoya *hardware store*
keimusho *jail, prison*
kijiya *fabric store*
kōba, kōjō *factory*
kōban *police box (local police station)*
kōen *park*
kuriininguya *dry cleaner*
kusuriya *pharmacy*
kutsuya *shoe store*
kyōkai *church*
mise *store*
nikuya *butcher shop*
pan'ya *bakery*
resutoran, shokudō *restaurant*
   (o-)hashi *chopsticks*
   inshokuzei *food/drink tax*
   (o-)kanjō *the check/bill*
   kissaten *tea room, coffee shop*
   kokku *a cook*
   menyū *menu*
   noren *door curtain*
   ryōtei *exclusive Japanese restaurant*
   sābisuryō *service charge*
   (o-)shibori *towel to wipe hands & face*
   sobaya *noodle stand*
   sunakku *snack shop*
   sushiya *sushi shop, sushi bar*
   uētā, bōi *waiter*
   uētoresu *waitress*
   wain risuto *wine list*
   waribashi *disposable, split chopsticks*
sakanaya *fish store*
(o-)shiro *castle*
shōten[gai] *marketplace, market street*
sōko *warehouse*
sūpā[māketto] *supermarket*
tabakoya *tobacconist*
(o-)tera *Buddhist temple*

tokoya *barber shop*
toshokan *library*
yaoya *greengrocer, vegetable store*
yūbinkyoku *post office*
   atena *addressee, addressee's name*
   ehagaki *picture postcard*
   funabin *sea mail*
   fūtō *envelope*
   genkin fūtō *money-mailer envelope*
   hagaki *postcard*
   hizuke *date*
   jūsho *address*
   kakitome [no] *registered*
   kitte *stamp*
   kōkūbin *air mail*
   kozutsumi *package, parcel (postal)*
   kyokuin *postal clerk*
   posuto *(public) mailbox*
   sashidashinin *return address, addressor*
   shishobako *post office box*
   sokutatsu *special delivery, express mail*
   tegami *letter*
   yūbin *the mail*
   yūbinbako *mailbox (public or private)*
   yūbinbangō *zip code, postal code*
   yūbin chokin *postal savings account*
   yūbin kawase *postal money order*
   yūbin'uke *private mailbox*
   yūbin'ya[san] *mailman, postman*

KAIMONO *Shopping*

baibai *buying and selling, trade*
chūmon suru *to order*
genkin *cash*
haitatsu *delivery*
harau *to pay (money)*
[kurejitto] kādo *credit card*
kaimono [o] suru *to shop, go shopping*
kanjō *bill, check, accounting*
kau *to buy*
kogitte[chō] *check[book]*
kouriten *retail store*
(o-)kyakusan/sama *guest, customer, client*
mihon *sample*
nedan *price*
okane *money*
ōuridashi *big sale*
sēru *sale*
shōhin *goods, product*
(o-)tsuri *change*
uru *to sell*
waribiki *discount*

TSŪSHIN Communications

denshin *telegraph*
denwa *telephone*
  denwa bangō *telephone number*
  denwachō *telephone book*
  denwa o kiru *to hang up*
  denwa o kakeru/suru *to make a phone call*
  hanashichū *busy (phone line)*
  kōkanshu *operator*
  kōshū denwa *public phone*
  rusuban *no answer*
  rusuban denwa *answering machine*
hōsō *broadcast, broadcasting*
konpyūtā *computer*
manga *comic book, cartoon*
pāsokon *personal computer*
rajio *radio*
shinbun *newspaper*
terebi *television*
yūbin *the mail*
zasshi *magazine*

RYOKŌ, YUSŌ Travel, Transportation

basutei *bus stop*
chizu *map*
eki *[train] station*
deguchi *exit*
deru *to exit, depart*
dōri, tōri *road, street, highway*
hidari *left*
higashi *east*
hōmu *platform*
iriguchi *entrance*
jiyū seki *free seating, open seating*
jōkyaku *passenger*
kankō suru *to go sightseeing*
katamichi *one-way*
kin'enseki *no-smoking seat*
kippu *ticket*
kippu uriba *ticket booth*
kita *north*
kōkū [gaisha] *airline [company]*
kokugai, kokusai *international*
kokunai *domestic*
kūkō *airport*
kyūkō *express train*
magaru *to turn*
massugu *straight (ahead)*
migi *right*
minami *south*
nishi *west*

noriba *(taxi/bus) stop, boarding place*
norikaeru *to transfer (to another vehicle)*
norimono *vehicle*
  basu *bus*
  chikatetsu *subway*
  densha *electric train*
  fune *boat, ship*
  herikoputā *helicopter*
  hikōki *airplane*
  jidōsha, kuruma *automobile, car*
  jinrikisha *rickshaw*
  jitensha *bicycle*
  jōyōsha *passenger car*
  kisen *steam ship*
  kisha *steam train*
  kyūkyūsha *ambulance*
  ōtobai *motorcycle*
  ressha *railroad train*
  sanrinsha *tricycle*
  shōbōsha *fire truck*
  takushii *taxi*
  torakku *truck*
noru *to board/get on (a vehicle)*
ōfuku *round-trip*
oriru *to disembark/get off (a vehicle)*
ryokō [o] suru *to travel*
-sen *-line*
shinkansen *Bullet Train*
shiteiken *reserved ticket*
shiteiseki *reserved seat*
shuppatsu suru *to depart*
shūten *last stop, terminal point*
tetsudō *railroad*
tobu *to fly*
tōchaku *arrival*
tomaru *to stop over, stay*
tsuku *to arrive*
unten suru *to drive [a car]*
yoyaku suru *to reserve/make a reservation*
-yuki *[destination]-line*
zaseki *seat*

SEKAI The World

chikyū *earth, globe*
kuni *country*
  Amerika, Beikoku *America*
  Amerika Gasshūkoku *The U.S.A.*
  Aruzenchin *Argentina*
  Betonamu *Vietnam*
  Burajiru *Brazil*
  Chūgoku *China*
  Chūka Jinmin Kyōwakoku *People's*

Republic of China
Doitsu, Doichu *Germany*
Eikoku, Igirisu *England*
Ejiputo *Egypt*
Firipin *Philippines*
Furansu *France*
Gurēto Buriten Great Britain
Indo *India*
Indoneshia *Indonesia*
Iraku *Iraq*
Iran *Iran*
Isuraeru *Israel*
Itariya *Italy*
Kanada *Canada*
Kankoku *Korea*
Mekishiko *Mexico*
Minami Afurika Kyōwakoku *Republic of South Africa*
Nihon, Nippon *Japan*
Nyū Jiirando *New Zealand*
Oranda *Netherlands*
Perū *Peru*
Roshia *Russia*
Sauji Arabia *Saudi Arabia*
Suisu *Switzerland*
Supein *Spain*
Tai *Thailand*
Taiwan *Taiwan*
Toruko *Turkey*
minato *port, harbor*
sekidō *the equator*
shima *island*
tairiku *continent*
Afurika *Africa*
Ajia *Asia*
Chūkintō *Middle East*
Hokkyoku *North Pole*
Hokkyoku Chihō *The Arctic*
Hokubei, Kita Amerika *North America*
Nanbei, Minami Amerika *South America*
Nankyoku *South Pole*
Nankyoku Tairiku *Antarctica*
Ōsutoraria *Australia*
Yōroppa *Europe*
umi *ocean*
Chichūkai *Mediterranean Sea*
Indoyō *Indian Ocean*
Karibukai *Caribbean Sea*
Taiheiyō *Pacific Ocean*
Taiseiyō *Atlantic Ocean*
unga *canal*

SHIZEN   *Nature*

hama, kaigan *beach*
hana *flower*
bara *rose*
botan *peony*
himawari *sunflower*
hinagiku *daisy*
kiku *chrysanthemum* (national flower of Japan)
suisen *daffodil*
tanpopo *dandelion*
yuri *lily*
hatake *(cultivated) field*
hayashi, mori *forest, grove*
ike *pond*
iro *color*
aka, akai *red*
ao, aoi, burū *blue*
chairo *brown*
gin'iro *silver-colored*
kiiro, kiiroi *yellow*
kin'iro *gold-colored*
kuro, kuroi *black*
midori, midoriiro *green*
momoiro, pinku *pink*
murasaki, murasakiiro *purple*
orenjiiro, daidaiiro *orange-colored*
shiro, shiroi *white*
iwa *boulder*
jishin *earthquake*
kashi no ki *oak tree*
kawa *river*
kazan *volcano*
ki *tree*
kumo *cloud*
kusa *grass*
matsu *pine (tree)*
mizuumi *lake*
niwa *garden*
oka *hill*
onsen *hot spring, spa*
sabaku *desert*
saku *to bloom*
sakura *cherry tree*
shokubutsu *plants*
sora *sky*
ta, tanbo *rice paddy*
take *bamboo*
tani *valley*
tsuchi *earth, ground*
yama *mountain*
umi *ocean*

DŌBUTSU *Animals*

ahiru *duck*
buta *pig*
fukurō *owl*
hebi *snake*
hitsuji *sheep*
ikimono, seibutsu *living thing/creature*
inu *dog*
kaeru *frog*
kame *turtle*
kamome *seagull*
kangarū *kangaroo*
kingyo *goldfish*
kirin *giraffe*
kitsune *fox*
koi *carp*
koinu *puppy*
konchū *insects*
  gokiburi *cockroach*
  hachi *bee*
  hae *fly*
  ka *mosquito*
  kabutomushi *Japanese beetle*
  kemushi *caterpillar*
  kirigirisu, inago *grasshopper, locust*
  kōrogi *cricket*
  kumo *spider*
  mushi *bug*
  semi *cicada*
  tonbo *dragonfly*
koneko *kitten*
kujaku *peacock*
kuma *bear*
naku *to call/cry/sing*
neko *cat*
nezumi *mouse, rat*
niwatori *chicken*
ōkami *wolf*
raion *lion*
risu *squirrel*
same *shark*
saru *monkey*
shichimenchō *turkey*
tanuki *badger*
tora *tiger*
tori *bird*
tsuru *crane*
uma *horse*
usagi *rabbit*
ushi *cow*
wani *alligator, crocodile*
washi *eagle*
yagi *goat*
zō *elephant*

Appendix A
The Japanese Writing System

Hiragana Syllabary

a あ	i い	u う	e え	o お
ka か	ki き	ku く	ke け	ko こ
ga が	gi ぎ	gu ぐ	ge げ	go ご
sa さ	shi し	su す	se せ	so そ
za ざ	ji じ	zu ず	ze ぜ	zo ぞ
ta た	chi ち	tsu つ	te て	to と
da だ	ji ぢ	zu づ	de で	do ど
na な	ni に	nu ぬ	ne ね	no の
ha は	hi ひ	fu ふ	he へ	ho ほ
ba ば	bi び	bu ぶ	be べ	bo ぼ
pa ぱ	pi ぴ	pu ぷ	pe ぺ	po ぽ
ma ま	mi み	mu む	me め	mo も
ya や		yu ゆ		yo よ
ra ら	ri り	ru る	re れ	ro ろ
wa わ				(w)o を
				n/n' ん

Hiragana Combination Characters

kya きゃ	kyu きゅ	kyo きょ	nya にゃ	nyu にゅ	nyo にょ
gya ぎゃ	gyu ぎゅ	gyo ぎょ	hya ひゃ	hyu ひゅ	hyo ひょ
sha しゃ	shu しゅ	sho しょ	bya びゃ	byu びゅ	byo びょ
ja じゃ	ju じゅ	jo じょ	pya ぴゃ	pyu ぴゅ	pyo ぴょ
cha ちゃ	chu ちゅ	cho ちょ	mya みゃ	myu みゅ	myo みょ
ja ぢゃ	ju ぢゅ	jo ぢょ	rya りゃ	ryu りゅ	ryo りょ

Katakana Syllabary

a	ア	i	イ	u	ウ	e	エ	o	オ
ka	カ	ki	キ	ku	ク	ke	ケ	ko	コ
ga	ガ	gi	ギ	gu	グ	ge	ゲ	go	ゴ
sa	サ	shi	シ	su	ス	se	セ	so	ソ
za	ザ	ji	ジ	zu	ズ	ze	ゼ	zo	ゾ
ta	タ	chi	チ	tsu	ツ	te	テ	to	ト
da	ダ	ji	ヂ	zu	ヅ	de	デ	do	ド
na	ナ	ni	ニ	nu	ヌ	ne	ネ	no	ノ
ha	ハ	hi	ヒ	fu	フ	he	ヘ	ho	ホ
ba	バ	bi	ビ	bu	ブ	be	ベ	bo	ボ
pa	パ	pi	ピ	pu	プ	pe	ペ	po	ポ
ma	マ	mi	ミ	mu	ム	me	メ	mo	モ
ya	ヤ			yu	ユ			yo	ヨ
ra	ラ	ri	リ	ru	ル	re	レ	ro	ロ
wa	ワ							(w)o	ヲ
								n/n'	ン

Katakana Combination Characters

kya	キャ	kyu	キュ	kyo	キョ	nya	ニャ	nyu	ニュ	nyo	ニョ
gya	ギャ	gyu	ギュ	gyo	ギョ	hya	ヒャ	hyu	ヒュ	hyo	ヒョ
sha	シャ	shu	シュ	sho	ショ	bya	ビャ	byu	ビュ	byo	ビョ
ja	ジャ	ju	ジュ	jo	ジョ	pya	ピャ	pyu	ピュ	pyo	ピョ
cha	チャ	chu	チュ	cho	チョ	mya	ミャ	myu	ミュ	myo	ミョ
ja	ヂャ	ju	ヂュ	jo	ヂョ	rya	リャ	ryu	リュ	ryo	リョ

Kanji

Pictographs

The earliest kanji were generally pictorial in origin, rough outlines of material objects they were intended to represent. Over the centuries they underwent gradual changes of form and lost their primitive pictorial appearance, as demonstrated below.

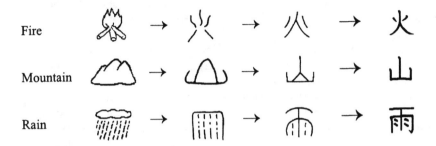

Fire

Mountain

Rain

Ideographs

Abstract concepts gradually found expression in the creation of ideographs to represent such things as numbers, directions, physical characteristics, and other concepts that could not be communicated using the more straightforward pictographs, as illustrated in these examples:

one	一	up, top	上	little	小
two	二	inside, center	中	white	白
ten	十	big	大	correct	正

Complex Characters

Both pictographs and ideographs are frequently employed in the construction of more complex characters:

木 → 森   日 + 月 → 明
tree   forest   sun   moon   light

門 + 耳 → 聞
gate   ear   hear, listen

On'yomi and Kun'yomi

Each kanji may be pronounced several different ways. The Japanese assigned a native pronunciation to each written character; however, they also employ the Chinese pronunciation–or nearest Japanese equivalent. This is particularly true for compound words, since the mono-syllabic Chinese language lends itself easily to the construction of compounds.

The Chinese reading for a kanji is called **on'yomi**, or "sound reading," while the Japanese pronunciation is **kun'yomi**, or "indigenous reading." These are often shortened to **on** and **kun**. Most of the 1,945 characters (**Jōyō Kanji**) currently recommended for daily use by the Japanese Language Council have both **on** and **kun** readings; however, over 700 have only **on'yomi** and about 35 have only **kun'yomi**.

Compound words are written with two or more kanji, usually pronounced the Chinese way. Occasional compounds may be pronounced by **kun'yomi** (eg. **tegami** *[letter]* = **te** *[hand]* + **kami** *[paper]*, both Japanese readings) or by a combination (eg., **yonjū** *[forty]*, where **yon** is **kun** and **jū** is **on**).

In a typical kanji reference book, when kana is used to indicate readings, the **kun'yomi** is written in hiragana and the **on'yomi** in katakana. There may be multiple possibilities for each, or there may be only one **on** and/or one **kun**. A few examples are shown below. For convenience, all readings are given in **rōmaji**, with **on** in capital letters and **kun** in lower case. **Okurigana** (kana that follows a kanji to indicate verb and adjective endings) and alternative pronunciations of the same readings are given in parentheses, and English meanings are shown in italics.

本	**HON (BON, PON)** **moto**	*origin, basis; book; counter* *for long, cylindrical objects*
日	**JITSU; NICHI (ni-, nit-)** **-ka; hi (bi, pi)**	*sun, day, daytime, counter for days*
山	**SAN (ZAN)** **yama**	*mountain, Mt.*
生	**SEI (ZEI), SHŌ (JŌ)** **i(-kiru); u(-mu; -mareru);** **ki; nama**	*to live; to give birth, be born; pure,* *genuine; raw; birth, life*
下	**KA, GE** **shita (jita); moto; shimo** **(jimo); kuda(-ru, -saru);** **sa(-geru, -garu)**	*bottom, under, beneath; base; lower;* *to go down; to hang, to lower;* *inferior; latter*
才	**SAI**	*counter for years of age*

Radicals

Certain simple kanji characters or parts of characters are frequently repeated, often in slightly altered form, in other characters. These repeated parts, called "radicals," take seven distinct forms, shown below, along with examples of whole characters containing each form. The radical described at left is the bold-faced portion of the character.

Hen   Left portion of a character with two distinct sides

休 野

Kamae   The portion that encloses a central figure.

間 国

Tsukuri   The right side of a character with two distinct sides.

新 郡

Tare   A part that starts overhead and droops down the side.

屋 痴

Kanmuri   The "crown" that sits at the top of a character.

花 雲

Nyō / Nyū   Runs down the left side and underneath the character.

遊 起

Ashi   "Legs" that seem to support the upper part of the character.

見 黒

There are over 200 standard radicals. Kanji reference books usually include a section on radicals, and characters are often grouped according to the radicals they contain.

Familiarity with radicals helps in recognizing and remembering kanji. Also, there are occasions when even native Japanese may not understand each other in conversation because of the frequency of homonyms–words that sound alike but have different meanings. Knowing how to describe a character can help clarify meaning. Often, simply giving the name of the radical is the quickest way to get the meaning across.

Punctuation

Basic Japanese punctuation marks are as follows:

kuten   ｡ *(period)* Used only at the end of a sentence. Also called **maru**, meaning *"circle."*

tōten   ､ *(comma)* More flexible and loosely defined than the English comma, **tōten** are used to indicate a pause or to clarify meaning or structure.

The following are used more or less like their English counterparts::
kakko   ( ) [ ] < >   *(parentheses, brackets)*
kagi, kagikakko   「 」   *(quotation marks)*
nakaten   •   *(bullet)*

nakasen — *(dash)* and **namigata** ~ (This curved dash is used primarily to indicate "from ~ to [a time, place, number/quantity, etc.].")

There are occasions when the Japanese will use English quotation marks, question marks, exclamation points, etc.; however, hyphens, colons, and semi-colons are never used in Japanese script.

The marks above are shown as they would be used in horizontal writing. For vertical writing, certain alterations must be made, as shown in the comparison examples below.

一八四一年（天保十二年）、今の栃木県に生まれた田中正造は、「人間にとっていちばん大切なのは、正しく生きることだ」といったのです。

一八四一年〈天保十二年〉、今の栃木県に生まれた田中正造は、「人間にとっていちばん大切なのは、正しく生きることだ」といったのです。

Writing Numbers

Arabic numerals are most often used to write numbers, except in formal or historical documents, and in some other miscellaneous circumstances. Kanji is used when it is more convenient, appropriate, or consistent but are avoided when the number is so large as to be cumbersome. The kanji for "hundred," "thousand," "ten thousand," etc., are sometimes used instead of the zeroes following a large number, especially on price tags and in advertising.

Ex.: ３５０人 = 350 people

５０円 = 50 yen*

￥５万 = 50,000 yen*

*The international symbol for the yen is ￥, but the kanji is 円.

Appendix B

Holidays & Historical Data

JAPANESE PUBLIC HOLIDAYS

Jan. 1-3	**O-shōgatsu**	New Year's Holiday (**Ganjitsu** = New Year's Day)
Jan. 15	**Seijin no Hi**	Coming-of-age Day
Feb. 11	**Kenkoku Kinenbi**	National Foundation Day
Mar. 20	**Shunbun no Hi**	Spring Equinox
Apr. 29	**Midori no Hi**	Nature Day*
May 3	**Kenpō Kinenbi**	Constitution Day*
May 4	**Kokumin no Kyūjitsu**	Citizens' Day*
May 5	**Kodomo no Hi**	Children's Day*
Sep. 15	**Keirō no Hi**	Senior Citizen's Day
Sep. 23	**Shūbun no Hi**	Autumnal Equinox
Oct. 10	**Taiiku no Hi**	Sports Day
Nov. 3	**Bunka no Hi**	Culture Day
Nov. 23	**Kinrō Kansha no Hi**	Labor Day
Dec. 23	**Tennō Tanjōbi**	Emperor's Birthday

***Gōruden Uiiku** Golden Week: So named because it includes four national holidays, as starred above.

OTHER FESTIVALS

Jul. 7	**Tanabata**	Feast of Stars, a romantic holiday for young lovers.
mid-July	**O-bon**	Feast of Souls, to honor the spirits of the dead.
Feb. 3 or 4	**Setsubun**	Traditional beginning of Spring.
Mar. 3	**Hina Matsuri**	Doll Festival (for young girls).

HISTORICAL DATA

Yamato original name of Japan
Amaterasu Ōmikami legendary sun goddess, ancestor of Jinmu
Jinmu original Emperor of Japan
tennō emperor
shōgun generalissimo, military leader of Japan
Edo old name for Tokyo
Ashikaga family in power during the Muromachi Period
Heike (Taira) and **Genji (Minamoto)** two powerful clans that supported rival candidates for leadership of Japan during the Heian Period

Fujiwara   historically the most influential family in the Japanese aristocratic hierarchy

Tokugawa   the family in power during the Edo Period

HISTORICAL PERIODS

Jōmon Period   ca. B.C. 7000
Yayoi Period   ca. B.C. 300
Yamato Period   ca. A.D. 300
Asuka Period   A.D. 552-710
Nara Period   710-794
Heian Period   794-1191
Kamakura Period   1185-1333
Muromachi Period   1333-1568
Azuchi-Momoyama Period   1573-1603
Edo Period   1603-1868
Meiji Period   1868-1912
Modern Period   1912-present
  Taishō Era   1912-1925
  Shōwa Era   1926-1988
  Heisei Era   1989-present

Proverbs

Senri no michi mo ippo kara. *A journey of a thousand ri begins with the first step. (1 ri = 2.44 miles)*

Kyō dekiru koto o ashita made nobasu na. *Don't put off until tomorrow what you can do today.*

Ichi o kiite, jū o shiru. *Hear one, know ten. (A word to the wise is sufficient.)*

Sandome no shōjiki. *The third time's the charm.*

Tayori no nai no wa yoi tayori. *No news is good news.*

Saru mo ki kara ochiru. *Even monkeys fall from trees.*

Narau yori nare yo. *Practice makes perfect.*

Chiri mo tsumoreba, yama to naru. *Mountains are made from specks of sand.*

Hajime ga daiji. *The beginning is the important thing. (Well begun is half done.)*

Kaeru no ko wa kaeru. *A frog's son is a frog. (Like father, like son.)*

Owari yokereba, subete yoshi. *All's well that ends well.*

Deru kugi wa utareru. *The nail that sticks up with be pounded down.*

Iwanu ga hana. *Not saying is the flower. (Silence is golden.)*

Isogaba maware. *Make haste slowly. (Haste makes waste.)*

Neko ni koban. *A coin before a cat. (Pearls before swine.)*

Uma no mimi ni nenbutsu. *A prayer in the ears of a horse. (Water off a duck's back. / Preaching to the wind.)*

Shiranu ga hotoke. *Ignorance is bliss.*

Index